About the book

'One of the most brilliantly insightful and u ever read. This should be essential reading most from themselves and
Stephen D Mayers, Invento.

'This is so much more than a business book. This is about maintaining brilliant relationships, bringing out the very best in people and creating the conditions for great success.'
Scanes Bentley, Executive Chairman, Norman Broadbent Group

'I read David's book at a critical time in my life, when my ex-wife had just died. I wanted to support my four teenage sons through this deeply upsetting period. It helped me just when I most needed it. It has been transformative. I found that its wisdom is applicable to all of life's challenges, not just organisational leadership. I strongly urge you to read it.
Tony Ingleby, Leadership Coach and Dad

The Path to Engagement is an incredibly powerful step by step guide for people who want to create far greater passion, energy and optimism, in themselves and their teams. Have you noticed how some people can stay motivated, positive and happy for long periods of time, whilst others slip into cynicism, boredom, moods or moaning. It is well known that highly engaged individuals and teams dramatically out-perform their counterparts when it comes to profits, growth, innovation and customer satisfaction.
- Would you like to help people acquire a compelling sense of purpose and positivity?
- Would you like to know how to re-energize people that have become negative, bored or pessimistic?
- Are you interested in finding out how to release more of your own natural happiness and potential?

The Path of Engagement is about refining your gift for leadership and bringing out the very best in your self others.

About the author

David Coleman is an acknowledged expert in performance improvement, with 30 years experience, both as a director and an advisor to well-known international brands.

He has built a reputation for his thought leadership on 'staff engagement' and his unusual ability to draw out the latent potential within teams and individuals alike. He is best known for building exceptionally high-performing teams and making sure everyone enjoys the journey, especially when the going gets tough.

The Path to
Engagement

David A Coleman

Good Habits Limited

Copyright © 2016 by David A. Coleman
All rights reserved. This book or any portion thereof
may not be reproduced or used in any manner whatsoever
without the express written permission of the publisher
except for the use of brief quotations in a book review.
Published by Good Habits Limited
First Printing, 2016
ISBN 978-0-9935402-0-2

Acknowledgements

I'd like to thank Ian 'Woody' Woodhouse, who helped co-create some of the key ideas in this book. Our friendship has been a truly creative gift.

I'd also like to thank my friends Tony Ingleby, Chilli Charlie and Catherine Llewelyn, who spent many long hours correcting my language and providing input on structure and readability. Thanks, I really appreciate it.

Finally I'd like to acknowledge that the spelling in this book is designed for an international readership. British readers will be horrified to see a 'z' where 's' should be. Likewise, our US friends will see 'u's in words like colour, where they shouldn't. I suggest we all see this as an exercise in accommodation and inclusion.

For my wife Sylvie

Contents

Big me, little me	1
The Beginnings of Engagement	6
The Why of Engagement	11
The States of Engagement	19
Fully Engaged	*21*
Opposition	*29*
Drama	*31*
The full Model	*32*
The Emotions of Engagement	*34*
The Spirit of Engagement	43
Labels everywhere	*44*
Rapport	*51*
Knowing the Score	*57*
The Great Circle	*65*
Motive	*75*
The Heart of Engagement	85
When Motive goes Bad	*86*
Selflessness	*90*
The Language of Engagement	93
Inspiration	*97*
Going 'Above the Line'	*102*
The Conditions for Engagement	107
A 'Why' Upgrade	*120*
Comfort Zones	*129*
The Art of Engagement	161
Resources	164

Big me, little me

I have always been aware that I can be two different people.

There's the me when I'm really firing on all 8 cylinders; I feel bright, open, naturally happy and making things happen seems effortless and fun. There's also the me that occasionally runs on one or two cylinders; I can become distracted, defensive, disillusioned, suspicious and sometimes the very master of procrastination or cynicism. I see this in other people as well, the signs are quite obvious. You must have seen this too.

Some people seem to hang on to their positive, happy, optimistic side for long periods of time. My mum seems to have done this for most of her life, quite an amazing feat. Other people seem to spend unhealthy amounts of time lingering in a less joyful place, only occasionally coming up for air.

From my own experience, most of us seem to spend the majority of our time swinging between the two, with the odd visit to each of the extremities. Certainly in my business life, I see this happening everywhere I look. Some teams seem able to joyfully match any challenge that's thrown at them, whilst others seem to specialize in boredom, complaining or moaning. I've spent considerable time in both types of team. It's like two different worlds.

I've also witnessed some managers become really good leaders and forge great depths of loyalty and commitment, where others seem to build a deadening conformity, create unnecessary frustration or even inspire passive rebellion. I'm sure we've all seen supposedly 'difficult people' suddenly come to life under a new manager and conversely, have seen top performers 'lose it' or fade away.

What makes people change like that? What makes a team fly or wallow in the mud? Why do I and other people feel engaged in one situation and turned off in another?

The purpose of this book is to provide a clear explanation as to what causes this and perhaps more importantly, what you can practically do to create far greater engagement.

If I'm honest, I like to think of myself as a reasonably resilient, positive and self-motivated person. However, the truth is, I am also deeply affected by the situations I find myself in and the circumstances and events that happen in my life. Positive environments and relationships rub off on me to great effect. I am invigorated, enlivened and encouraged by them. The trouble is, negative ones rub off on me too. I know they shouldn't, but they do.

I'd like to admit up front, I'm not from the school of simply blocking out the negative and only focusing on the positive. I think to do that, you have to stop feeling anything at a certain level and I don't want to do that. In my experience, if you cut out the lows through growing a thick skin, you also cut out the highs. I don't want a thick skin. Thick skins lead to dull senses and dull minds. If anything, I want to increase my awareness and refine my senses, whilst managing difficulty more intelligently.

On the work front, I've noticed the huge impact engagement has on a broad spectrum of important elements: performance, creativity, colleagues and customers. It can be the difference between a good or a great company, the line between failure or success or, in more human terms, loving your job or just hating it.
This book is for anyone that is interested in transforming or improving that mood or atmosphere, whether it be at a personal, team or company-wide level.

The closest word that describes what I'm referring to is 'Engagement', the extent to which you love what you do and are fully absorbed and enthused by it.

I've held off a bit from linking engagement to supercharged performance, at this early stage. Don't get me wrong, as we shall soon see in a couple of chapters, there is undeniable, proven evidence that improved engagement leads to dramatically improved performance, across a broad spectrum of measures.

However, if you set about trying to improve engagement, but in reality, all you are really interested in is more profit, greater innovation or higher productivity, your spells won't work.

The great wizard Merlin, of Arthurian legend, revealed a universal truth when he said to Arthur 'The King and the Land are one'. This wisdom can be equally applied to the nature of engagement itself. You can't fake it, you've actually got to give it to receive it.

In the same way, if you pretend to have rapport with someone, they will see through it, consciously or unconsciously and keep you at arms length. Rather than refine our pretending skills, let's work on our liking skills and our ability to let people in. The door to your house opens inwards, not outwards. This is the essence to the path of engagement.

I believe within all of us lie deep reservoirs of positivity, potential and a desire to make a difference. Our natural state is to be collaborative, interested, enthusiastic, playful and bright. You only have to look at children playing or people doing what they love best to get a sense of that. No midwife has ever delivered a baby and said "I'm sorry madam, this is a negative baby, but don't worry, it will get a good management job later on". That just doesn't happen. You don't have to take lessons in joy or happiness. It's already there. Sometimes it gets buried or covered up and we need a little help to polish it up again. People arrive on the planet positive and ready to go... and then stuff happens.

I've been very lucky in my life. I've had more than my fair share of mentors and teachers along the way. The purpose of this book is to pass on some of their magic and wisdom and explore how to enrich our own lives and the lives of those around us.
In truth, most of my teachers never knew they were teachers, especially the best ones. They just happen to be brilliant at leading positive lives that profoundly effect everyone they come into contact with. Their 'mood' certainly rubbed off on me and I shall remain forever grateful. You will be introduced to them shortly within the pages of this book.

The first chapter examines how we seem to have the ability to experience so many moods, states of mind and differing abilities to remain positive. How is it that some people get over things quickly and others use the same experience to have a year-long sulk? How come diets, or 'changes in lifestyle' as we say these days, are logically the way to lose weight, but are emotionally so difficult to adhere to? How come some people seem to be able to keep going under difficult circumstances and others fall back on blaming others for their circumstances or less resourceful ways of dealing with hardship?

Perhaps most interesting of all, how is it that some people can reach the age of eighty and still shine with the glee of a youngster and others seem old and tired before they have even hit thirty?

I know from general knowledge and a sustained interest in the subject, that genetics, medical pre-dispositions and early formative experiences all play their part in our mood and psychological outlook. However, without doubt, something else seems to be influencing our moods and our level of engagement, happiness and well-being.

We all know or have heard of people that were not necessarily dealt a good hand of cards at birth or later on in life, but shone through. Likewise, we know of people that 'had it on a plate', but never really made the most of their privileged start. It's more than just toughness or the lack of it. So what is it?

The second chapter, 'The Why of Engagement', explores the stunning impact engagement, or the lack of it, can have on our ability to perform and excel, individually or collectively. For those readers that are less interested in the commercial aspect of engagement, you can either skim or skip this chapter. Having said that, the powerful effect deeper engagement has on business performance is equally visible in personal relationships, it's just that we tend not to measure it. One thing is for certain, however, the astonishing uplifts that can be achieved in profitability, innovation or customer satisfaction, can equally be achieved in happiness, spontaneity and romance.

There have been many studies on the subject and I shall be referring to some of the more extensive and credible ones. Pleasingly, what is immediately clear is that the level of concurrence between these studies is very high, adding real authenticity to our conclusions. The amount of data available on this subject is unsurprisingly colossal and almost impossible to get your arms around all of it. I have attempted to summarize that data on a few short pages and draw out some of the primary findings. I hope you will find this section both interesting and informative.

The following chapters go directly into the causes of engagement and disengagement. The primary focus is on how to use this understanding to improve our own engagement levels and the engagement of those around us. Some of the answers to this puzzle are straight-forward and intuitive. Some of the skills are an art and take time to develop. Either way, they are more than worth the investment, as the payback can be tremendous.

As mentioned before, I have had more than my fair share of mentors and teachers. There is one however, I'd like to mention in person.

His name is Ian 'Woody' Woodhouse. I had the privilege of owning a business with Ian for ten years. It was during that time that we developed, refined and passed on many of the key ideas and insights laid out in the following pages. Woody is one of the most insightful and funniest people I have ever met and I hope I have captured some of his genius in this book.

I have worked in a number of well known organisations, both as a director, executive coach and facilitator for front-line managers and coaches. I have found these principles apply equally well in both a personal and a business context. In particular, I have seen them contribute to significant leaps in performance, creativity and most importantly, to the happiness levels of those that gave them a go.

This book is written for you. It is not limited to the you at work, the you at home, the you with friends or even the you alone. It is written for the you that is present in all those roles. I have drawn on examples from commerce and others that are more personal in nature. They both have the same message for us. 'Greater engagement rejuvenates, enriches, emboldens and inspires'. This book is about creating more.

Like all efforts to improve things at an essential level, the true beneficiary of this book of course won't just be you. As Woody would often say, 'the real beneficiaries should be your partners, your family, your colleagues and the people you are yet to meet'.

The Beginnings of Engagement

In 1860, at the meeting of the British Association in Oxford, Charles Darwin, the celebrated natural scientist, suggested something so shocking and so sacrilegious that Lady Brewster fainted and bishops railed against it with bibles raised above their heads. What could possibly have caused such offence and a ruffling of cassocks and feathers?!

As we all now know, the suggestion was that we all share a common ancestor and that we are descended from apes. In fact, Darwin went much further in his publication of 'The Origin of Species', where he laid out the process of evolution itself and the process through which evolution is achieved.

In its simplest form, he proposed that man is descended from apes, apes from mammals, mammals from reptiles, reptiles from amphibians and amphibians from fish, all the way back to plants. The process responsible for this transformation was 'natural selection', making countless incremental improvements over long, long periods of time, culminating in present-day mankind.

This brilliant insight created a vast leap in our understanding and made us rethink our place in the world. Naturally, the idea that humans shared a common ancestor with apes was a challenge to the foundations of thinking at the time, probably on a par with Galileo's proofs of a sun-centered world a hundred years before him.
You may well ask, what has this got to do with engagement? Well, as it happens, rather a lot!

As we progressed through our various stages of evolution, our brain followed a parallel path of development. Most importantly, as the earlier structures of our reptile and mammalian brains had proven their effectiveness, there was no reason for them to be discarded. In fact, quite the opposite. Evolution seems to have favoured a process of building additional layers of our brains on top of existing structures, rather than rebuilding everything from scratch.
This has huge implications for us. Not only do we have our newer human brain, but this lies wrapped and entangled around a much older, more primitive, instinctual mind.

The good news is this means we have three brains. The bad news is that they don't always agree with each other! Prof. Steve Peters explains this beautifully in his brilliant book 'The Chimp Paradox'. A good, although approximate, model for understanding the brain in terms of its evolutionary history is the famous 'triune brain theory' created by Paul MacLean (see figure 1). The main idea is that three distinct brains emerged one after the other in the course of our evolution, which now co-inhabit our human skull:

The **reptilian** brain, the oldest and deepest of the three, controls the body's vital functions such as heart rate, breathing, body temperature and balance.

The **limbic** brain subsequently emerged in the first mammals. It is thought to be responsible for feelings and emotions and has a powerful capacity to read body language and sense the intentions of others (important if you want to identify who wants to eat you or not). The limbic brain is the seat of our decision-making (often unconscious or hidden from our more modern human brain) and exerts a powerful influence over our behavior. Profound feelings such as trust, needs, desires and fears emanate from this centre.

The **neocortex**, our newest brain, first assumed importance in primates and culminated in the human brain with its two large cerebral hemispheres. These hemispheres have been responsible for the development of language, logic, abstract thought, imagination, and consciousness. The neocortex is unimaginably flexible and has almost infinite learning abilities. The neocortex is what has enabled human cultures to develop and has produced the explosion of progress we have seen in the modern world today. Two million years ago we were apemen. Today we are spacemen. That is the power and the beauty of the neocortex.

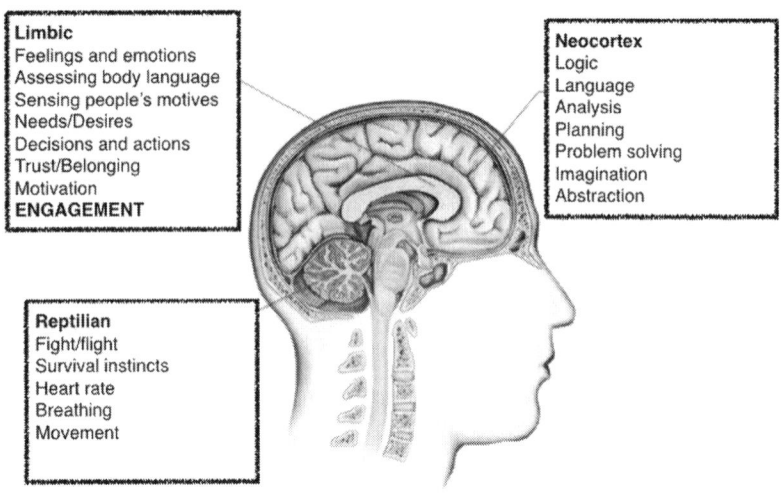

(Figure 1 The triune brain)

So why the science lesson and what has this got to do with the subject of Engagement? If the three brains all agreed with each other and shared common objectives and motivations, there would be no need to mention it. The trouble is, quite often they don't and that's where the fun starts!

The three parts of our brain do not operate entirely independently of one another. They have established numerous interconnections through which they influence, negotiate, argue and in many cases try to undermine each other. Without doubt though, despite the brilliance of the neocortex, the limbic brain has the upper hand.

You don't have to be a clever scientist to work this out, you just have to put yourself on a diet and watch what happens: Shortly after the commencement of your diet, you will notice that strange things start to happen. Firstly, time itself starts to stretch, the gap between meals becomes unimaginably long. After twenty four hours, biscuits and chocolate start to grow legs and try to gain illegal entry into your mouth. The more you say to yourself 'don't think of food', the more you seem to become obsessed by it. If you make it to the end of the week, it may all end in tears with a huge 'fridge raid', rapidly followed by sincere and heart felt promises of 'we'll start it properly tomorrow'.

In the same way, the smoker trying to quit faces the same struggle. The logical neocortex reads the back of the packet; 'Smoking Kills'. It doesn't say smoking may give you a mild cold, no, it actually says 'Smoking Kills'. Nevertheless, all it takes is a moment of distraction, a little stress or a glass of wine and before you you know it, you are opening the packet and reaching for the cure. In fact, it's often worse than that. Your voice of reason can be saying 'don't do it, you won't even enjoy it, this is madness' but at the same time you observe yourself doing all the actions required to get that death-stick in your mouth and light it. This is the work of the limbic brain. Logic has little defence against desire or need!

Welcome to the limbic brain, not that it needs any introduction. We are all familiar with it and know it well.

Experiencing total commitment, feeling part of something incredibly special, loving what you are doing, feeling deeply motivated, all lie in the realm of the Limbic mind, out of the reach of logic or reason. Engagement is not logic, it's Limbic!

You can't force engagement, demand it, order it, mandate it, convince people of it, or trick people into it. It has a mind of its own. Literally.

Engagement would also seem to be the natural state. It is not something learnt, but something we arrived with. You see it most strongly in children, in people passionate about what they are doing, or sports people competing at the highest level. Consider kids playing, or your own recollections from your childhood. I've got strong memories of cardboard boxes being transformed into rockets, or sticks and dustbin lids becoming swords and shields, as I embarked on some imaginary quest. Engagement is innate, it's something we arrived with, a quality that is always there, deep within us.

You can't force or impose it upon others, but you can inspire it and can certainly create the conditions for it to emerge.

If you are lucky, you may encounter someone on your journey that can draw out these special qualities that lie deep within you, someone that can see your potential and coax it to the surface for all to see, someone that shines a light on you that is brighter than the one you shine on yourself. I know what it feels like to be fully engaged, I know how creative and alive I am capable of being. You know how that feels too. I also know what I'm like when I feel the opposite. It's as if I'm two entirely different people.

This book is about the skills, the science and to a great degree, the art of transforming your own engagement levels and the engagement levels of those around you.

In the world of engagement, they say EQ is more important than IQ. Let's explore this world and see if we can get her to give up some of her secrets. Before we do that, let's examine the link between engagement and productivity, its impact on creativity and even its consequences for personal well-being. I think you'll find the numbers eye-opening, if not shocking. I certainly did.

The Why of Engagement

In this chapter, we will explore the tremendous impact engagement can have on individuals, teams and organisations. I have drawn on a number of sources including; a significant survey performed by the Gallup Organisation and the now well-known 'MacLeod Report', produced for the UK government by David MacLeod and Nita Clarke (Crown copyright).

The numbers below were derived from a survey by Gallop of over 23,910 business units in the UK, comprising both large corporates right across the spectrum to smaller and medium sized businesses. This is a statistically significant sample size and makes the findings worthy of due consideration. Gallup have since conducted a similar survey in the US during 2014, tracking 80,837 employed adults. They uncovered a very similar spread of engagement levels.

Profit
Companies in the top quartile of engagement scores achieve **twice the annual net profit** of those in the bottom quartile

This is a very big number and must represent many millions if not billions on the bottom line. Many senior executives allow their attention to be consumed with 'shareholder satisfaction' and ensuring a good rate of return is achieved. This in turn, has a considerable impact on what gets talked about and focused on in the boardroom. I know from personal experience, that cost reduction and revenues are very much top of most agendas. Quite often, matters of staff and even customer satisfaction barely get a look-in and if they do, only as a reported metric.

I understand that pressure, I have felt it myself, it's constant and daunting. Shareholder satisfaction is a very real dynamic at a senior level. However, it's quite clear from the evidence that better profits are afforded to those organisations that truly value engagement and genuinely spend time and resources to nurture it. What does your organisation talk about in the boardroom?

Revenue growth
Organisations in the top quartile of engagement scores demonstrated **revenue growth 2.5 times greater** than those in the bottom quartile.

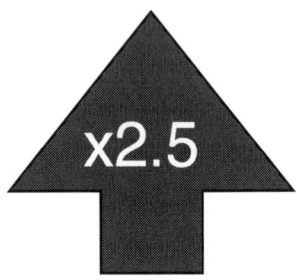

As markets get increasingly competitive, aggressive and globalized, that's a huge advantage by any stretch of the imagination. That sort of growth only happens when customers want what you've got and really like the way you give it to them. The link between engaged staff and how that makes customers feel must be a key piece of the puzzle. Some companies have high emotional appeal, others don't. Some of this is branding, a lot of it is down to the level of engagement housed within a business.

Innovation
59% **of engaged employees said that their job brings out their most creative ideas**, against 3% of those less engaged

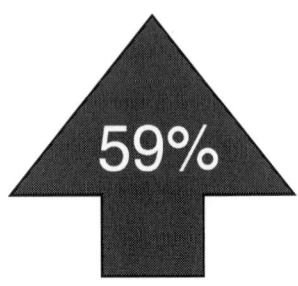

As we continue deeper into the digital age, innovation is becoming increasingly critical. Whilst it's no surprise that engaged people feel more creative and feel able to be more creative, the real question is how do you evoke that sort of creativity in the first place? What gets in the way of innovation, what stops people from having good ideas? What makes people bring their 'light bulbs' to the table and bother doing more than just the minimum?

Productivity

Organisations in the top quartile of employee engagement scores have **18% higher productivity** than those in the bottom quartile.

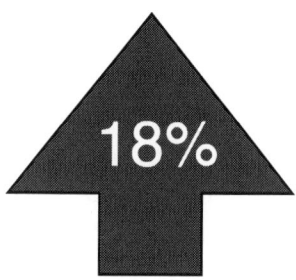

18% might not seem a lot, but as any finance guy will tell you, it has huge implications for the bottom line, especially if you have large operation or production areas. I'm not at all surprised by this figure, even if I look at my own productivity levels when I'm either engaged or not. Big difference! I'm sure we're all a bit like that.

Employee turnover

Companies with high levels of engagement show **staff turnover rates 40% lower** than companies with low levels of engagement.

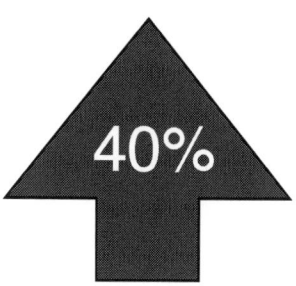

I don't have your figures to hand, but I bet if you looked at those people who felt disengaged then left, I suspect they were the brighter, more adventurous types. Knowhow and high performers are a key asset to any business. Hanging on to them has got to be a priority. High staff turnover is a very costly business, not just financially with the need for additional recruitment and retraining, but also the loss of know-how, quality customer interaction and pride in the business.

'People join companies and leave bosses' as the saying goes. Engagement plays a big part in that.

Customer advocacy
Companies with top quartile engagement scores average **12% higher customer advocacy**.

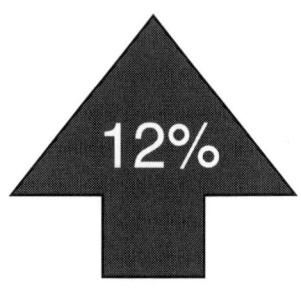

I'm going to stick my neck out. As you can see, I've put customer advocacy last. The reason I've done this isn't because I think customers are not important, they are. Without customers you don't have a business, you don't have anything. However, and this is a central theme I'd like to explore, engaged staff is the very thing that builds customer advocacy in the first place.

Staff engagement is causal and is the precursor to customer advocacy

Customer advocacy is the **result** of how well you listened to what your customers wanted, how well you designed your service or product to fulfil that need, how well you delivered that service and how well you cleared up the mess if anything went wrong. How well you do all of that, boils down to how much and how well your staff **want** to do all of that.

Since the first posters were pinned to walls in offices in the early 80's hailing 'The Customer is King', up until the present day, there has been a relentless focus, if not obsession with the customer. It would seem that we have arrived at a point where customers have become more important than the people serving them. I believe this is wrong and will lead to a poorer result than could otherwise be achieved.

Most if not all companies are striving to be ever increasingly customer-centric. Smarter companies are offering increasingly personalized services and increasing numbers of channels that customers can chose (telephone, web, social, mobile, face-to-face etc). Ease is becoming the prime metric for forward thinking companies, as customers want ever increasing simplicity and immediacy.

Don't get me wrong, I think that's a good thing. However, those companies that are really moving ahead and stealing a march on their competition, have moved to a higher level. They recognize that what is wanted isn't just customer focus, it's **People focus**.

People focus includes both staff and the customer and sets a more enlightened balance to achieve far more.

Engagement is a true differentiator. However, you can't force it, demand it, order it, mandate it, trick people into it or even buy it. Engagement is something that is given, not taken. Engagement is something that emerges and arises when the conditions are right.

Let's have a look at what some people said during these studies:

'Company accounts that show the workforce as a cost on the balance sheet, alongside capital depreciation, encourage a boardroom mindset which ignores the people factors'.
Will Hutton, Executive Vice Chair of the Work Foundation

'...was shocked when he realized that the company knew more about its customers than it did about its employees'.
Terry Leahy Tesco Chief Executive

'There is an increasing understanding that people are the source of productive gain, which can give you competitive advantage'.
Tim Besley, Economist, member of the Monetary Policy Committee

'When I started this journey, people thought I was mad and the Board were not universally enthused. But I knew that without getting the workforce fully engaged and committed, the company would die. Instead of which it was reborn'.
Garvis Snook, Director ROK

Individual level perspective
Assuming the average person starts work at 18 years old and finishes these days at around 58 and spends an average of 39.2 hours per week (five weeks holiday a year factored in), you will work 92,120 hours in a life time. Oh, and that's paid hours and doesn't include the commute. That's a lot of time, particularly if much of it is experienced as feeling disengaged, frustrated, bored or underutilized.

In the 2013 Aon Hewitt Database global survey, only 19% of people in work in Europe felt highly engaged. Disturbingly, an equal number, 19%, scored themselves as actively disengaged. The report describes 'actively disengaged' as those employees who are 'actively destroying value through negativity'. In its US survey during 2014, Gallup determined that 17.5% of staff were actively disengaged.

In a report produced by Towers Perrin, it states that only 29 per cent of UK employees believed their senior managers were sincerely interested in their well-being; only 31 per cent thought their senior managers communicated openly and honestly; only three per cent thought their managers treated them as key parts of the organisation and no fewer than 60 per cent felt their senior managers treated them as just another organisational asset to be managed.

The Sainsbury Centre for Mental Health point to the loss of productivity for those who are ill but still in work; they estimate the cost due to mental ill-health alone is £15 billion a year.

Engaged employees in the UK take an average of 2.69 sick days per year; the disengaged take 6.19. The CBI reports that sickness absence costs the UK economy £13.4 billion a year.

Gallup also point to the negative effects of disengagement. Fifty-four per cent of the actively disengaged say that work stress caused them to behave poorly with friends or family members in the previous three months, against 17 per cent of the engaged. More alarmingly, 54 per cent of the actively disengaged say their work lives are having a negative effect on their physical health, versus 12 per cent of the engaged.

Enough numbers, I get it!
I think that's probably enough statistics, surveys and reports for now. However, I hope it helps to clarify just how big a deal engagement is, whether that be at a personal, corporate or country level. Get it right

and the prize is huge. Get it wrong and you will be forever wondering where the hole in the bucket is. I know quite a few companies that are scratching their heads over this. Is yours?

From my own experience, of all the things you can do to improve performance, the biggest leaps emerge when groups of people collectively choose to fully engage and go for it. This doesn't just apply to work, we see it in all fields of life.

Much of this information is now in the public domain. For further reading, I strongly suggest that you delve further into the McLeod report and it's findings. It is widely read and well understood in HR circles. I would like to lend my support in promoting it to a larger audience.   A particularly good website to visit is http://engageforsuccess.org, they have organized the information between engagement and performance particularly well.

Before we get ahead of ourselves, let's have a much closer look at engagement itself and our own relationship with it. For me, there have certainly been periods when I have felt deeply engaged and very much alive. To be honest, there have also been periods when I have felt bored, stuck in a routine, feeling like I'm not really going anywhere, directionless or flat. Under these circumstances only a beer and a good moan will do! Ideally, this should be with someone that absolutely agrees with how wrong everyone else is and, more importantly, how right I am!! I think we've all been there.

How can we stay on the positive side, how can we keep that going and how can we help those around us stay on that path?

Shall we begin?

The States of engagement

'He's with the bank you know'
If you ask a group of people or anyone for that matter, when they feel most engaged, they will usually tell you:

'When I'm doing something I'm interested in'
'When I"m doing something linked to my personal goals'
'When I'm at home with my children, just playing'
'When I'm learning something'
'When I'm with friends'
'When I'm being praised or recognized for something'

I think all of these are true and all of us have experienced these from time to time. There is however, a universal experience we all seem to share regarding feeling engaged, and that has got to do with a simple thing called… **'When something's new'**.

Certainly, if I look at my own experience, I have always been particularly engaged when something is new, whether that be a relationship, a job, or even a car or a new hobby. Let me explain.

In 2004, I was invited to join a well known international bank, as Head of Global Contact Centres and was based in Hyderabad, India for three years. 12,500 staff, fifteen centres, in five countries. Wow, that was quite a step up for me. This was my first proper big role. I was more proud than pride itself. My shoes had more polish on them than they had had in the whole of the previous year. My tie was tied to a perfect triangle and everyone I met got an extra special good energy 'good morning'. Because it and I were new. I didn't have to drag myself out of bed, I was lifted out of bed as if by an invisible thread. I didn't have to go to work, I wanted to go to work.

I felt nervous and excited and overflowing with energy. If on my first day, I was told that my office was no longer going to be the big one in the corner, as we are moving to an open floor format, it wouldn't have been a problem at all. I'm positive, flexible and generous. If it works for the good of the whole, count me in. I'd probably be asking 'Would you like some help moving my stuff?' Because it's new and I feel 100% engaged and willing. This even rubbed off on my dear mother. She's just as excited with my news and is now telling all of her friends 'He's with the bank you know'. All is good.

The same is true with relationships. When I first met Sylvie, my wife, boy was I engaged. I was making her cups of tea, not because she asked for it. No, no, no, I was making her cups of tea just because I thought she'd love it. When she spoke, I hung off every word, I was fully listening to every syllable she uttered, deeply curious, deeply interested. I felt a strong sense of gratitude and a natural sense of optimism. The weekend hasn't even happened yet...but I already know it's going to be brilliant.

If she ever said 'Can I have a cup of tea?', I'd apologize for my lack of anticipation and she'd soon get the tea, plus biscuits on the side. Keep that sort of thing going for any period of time and you may even find yourself pulling out a ring and actually getting engaged. I did!! Brilliant.

This experience seems to relate to things as well. When we move into a new house or maybe get a new kitchen, we start to make ourselves promises. Things like 'this worktop will always be kept spotless'. 'This oven will always be kept clean!' or 'the spare bedroom will never be used as a dumping ground'.

You can always tell when someone, guys in particular, gets a new car. It may not necessarily be brand new, but it's new to them. As he walks away from it, he always does the same thing, after the fifth, six or seventh pace. He'll turn round to have a look, to get that 3/4 view and then continue on with a skip in his feet and a prideful wobble of the head. Again, he would have made the same promises. 'This car will always be kept in pristine condition', 'My car will never have muddy boots in it'. If you don't believe me, try getting in to a friends new car with muddy boots. I'll be very surprised if you don't get that 'don't even think about it' look.

We've all got stories and experiences of what things are like when things are new. It's like you are on a journey to somewhere great. I call it **'The Path to Engagement'**. Given the option, I wouldn't want to do anything else.

I love what I'm doing and I'm doing what I love.

States of Engagement

Here is a list of how people tell me they feel and what they experience when they are fully on this path. We've all felt these things, these emotions are not strangers to us.

Remember, it's the emotions that drive engagement.

Fully Engaged
Great energy
Gratitude
Excited
Positive
Enthusiastic
Optimistic
Happy
Interested
Curious
Focused
Generous
Kind
Collaborative
Proud
Confident

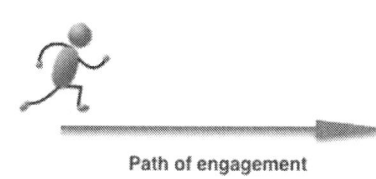

Path of engagement

(figure 1 - The path of engagement)

That is a fantastic set of feelings. People would pay a lot of money to feel that, some try to! Wouldn't it be great if we could keep that going for much longer periods of time. The trouble is, life is life and sometimes we get delivered 'Events'. Thankfully some of these events make it even easier to stay on that path. Other events have completely the opposite effect.

I'd like to have a much closer look at these 'events' and how we respond to them. They seem to play a central role in our states of engagement. Let's say my boss at the bank writes an email to his boss and copies me in;

To: Alan
From: Rob
cc: David

Re: David Coleman

Hi Alan
Just a short note to say in his first month David has already implemented a couple of great initiatives which seem to already be bearing fruit. I'm delighted we took him on and I look forward to further progress.
Rob

There I was all excited and enthusiastic and now I'm even more pumped up and looking forward to doubling my efforts. Great, life is good. I'm even looking forward to telling my Mum and Dad.

Many events are not so positive, in fact, quite the opposite:

Imagine Sylvie and I have been invited to the annual tennis club summer dance. We have been looking forward to it for weeks and finally we are here. Everything was great until I just happened to notice that Sylvie is dancing far more enthusiastically with the tennis coach than she ever was with me. Ouch! That's an event!

I was told at my interview that the company values fairness, equal opportunity and promotion based on merit and achievement. It soon becomes clear my boss has favourites... and I'm not one of them. I'd hit all of my targets but was told I didn't get invited to interview for potential promotion because I apparently lacked a previously undiscussed quality called 'gravitas'. That's an event!

I've gone shopping at a supermarket to find someone has backed into my car and has left an appreciable dent. No note, no apology, just a big dent. That's an event!

All these things make it harder to stay in that positive mode and to remain in that magical, pristine state of engagement. This is a very important moment, although it's easy to miss. In the heat of the moment, not many of us recognize that when we get delivered an event, we have also simultaneously hit a **decision point.** (figure 2)

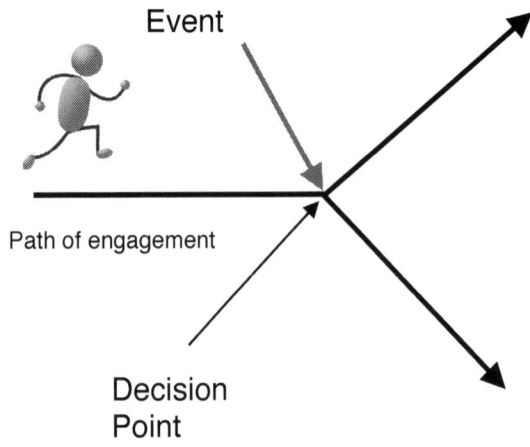

(Figure 2 - Decision Point)

Decision Points are far more obvious when we hit a 'Major Event'. The events are dramatic and feel very negative. Lesser events trigger far smaller levels of emotion and may only be experienced as thoughts.

Major events are easy to spot. They generate the big emotions of disdain, anger, revenge, self-pity, resignation or apathy. In addition to these strong feelings, the voice in your head can also get particularly outraged, hissy and 'stompy'. Not very good English I know, but that's what it feel like.

Imagine at the interview with the bank I was told that I had been successful in my application. I had been awarded the role of Head of Global Contact Centres; 12,500 staff, 15 centres and a region comprising 5 countries. I am feeling proud, optimistic and very clever indeed. On arrival in India, I am given some very unexpected news by the local country manager.

'David, as was undoubtedly explained at your interview, the Bank is undergoing considerable change at the moment. We currently have a companywide transformation programme underway, looking to restructure resources and organize ourselves towards a more appropriate and customer centric model. I'm sure you understand. I know this is slightly different from what was discussed at your interview, but we'd like you to initially look after the Hyderabad centre and the Hyderabad centre alone. We appreciate your flexibility in this matter and I've already taken the liberty, on your behalf, to instruct HR to draft up an amended contract for you to sign at your convenience. Welcome to India and welcome aboard!'

Well, that's not just any old event. That's a major event. When you hit a major event, it becomes obvious that you've hit a decision point and you have to make a choice of some sort.

Similarly, let's say I found out a week later that there was a reason Sylvie was dancing so enthusiastically with the tennis coach... and it wasn't just because he was a good dancer! (Don't worry, I'm just making this up!!)

This again would be a major event. They don't happen very often, thank goodness, but when they do, it's quite a jolt, even a life changer. In both imaginary examples, it's obvious I've been delivered a 'Major Event' and I've reached a decision point on my path. I can't just carry on and pretend nothing happened. It's obvious I have to do something and I have to make some choices. 'Another cup of tea dear?' isn't going to make this go away and is clearly not the solution.

In reality, if I'm to stay on the path and retain my values, my pride and my forward momentum, I've got a couple of simple choices.

Should I stay or should I go? (figure 3)

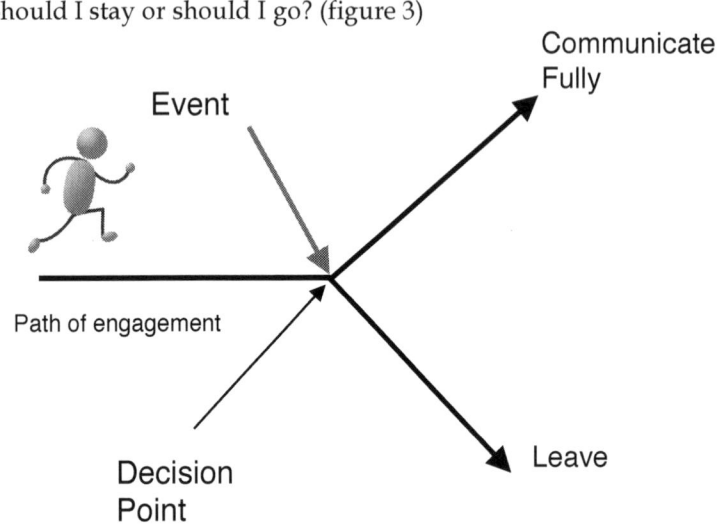

(Figure 3 - Should I stay or should I go)

In this instance, leaving is a perfectly honourable option. You promised me one thing in the interview and one flight later you are completely changing our agreement. I've only been here a couple of days and you are already breaking significant promises. Thanks but no thanks, I'm off somewhere else, to play a better game.

My other option is to stay, but to do that, we would need to what I call 'Communicate Fully'. In the instance with the imaginary episode with Sylvie, it would require a lot more than just saying 'I'm angry' and her saying she's sorry. I would need to really feel that she understands how much this has hurt me, angered me and made me question everything. I would need to understand what led up to this and how we got to this state. I would also have to hear some things from her I'd never given her the space to say before. I would need to admit and understand my part in the breakdown. It's likely some of these conversations would be best helped by a facilitator or by a third party, to ensure full listening and some balance was preserved in the discussion. It's possible to go through events like that and come out the other side and have a more resilient marriage, based on a deeper understanding of each others real needs.

My main point is, when a 'Major Event' gets delivered to you (or you bring one on yourself), it's obvious you have hit a decision point and you have to make a choice. You can't just 'keep calm and carry on'. Thankfully very few events are that dramatic, they are usually irritants, disappointments or misunderstandings.

The trouble with decision points is that they take us out of our comfort zones. Well outside. The Limbic Brain does not like this at all and goes into survival mode. This usually takes the form of finding excuses or reasons to avoid interacting with the issue. Anything to avoid leaving its comfort zone. This is partly where the problem lies. The limbic brain has very strong responses to comfort zones, based on our historical and animalistic roots. It equates leaving its comfort zone with very real physical danger or even mortality. This is why simple things for some people like public speaking, Karaoke in my case, or even saying hello to strangers, feels like a real threat, when in reality it is nothing like that at all.

The problem is, **whenever** you get delivered an event, however small, you are also presented with a decision point, whether you notice it or not. If an event isn't that significant, you may be presented with a bit of a dilemma. Let's say I did see Sylvie dancing more enthusiastically with the tennis coach than she was with me. I don't want to make a big fuss about it, as I will run the risk of being seen as a small, jealous little man, who jumps to silly conclusions and should be big enough to allow his woman to have a good time. At the same time, I also don't want to leave, as that would be too painful and anyway, I'm crazy about her. So, I'm not leaving and I'm not communicating. The decision point came and went and I avoided it and did nothing (other than moan to myself). Without realizing it, I'm now taking a path where no path exists. I have moved off the 'Path of Engagement' and am now entering a completely different state. I am taking the path of disengagement and it starts to feel very different. (figure 4)

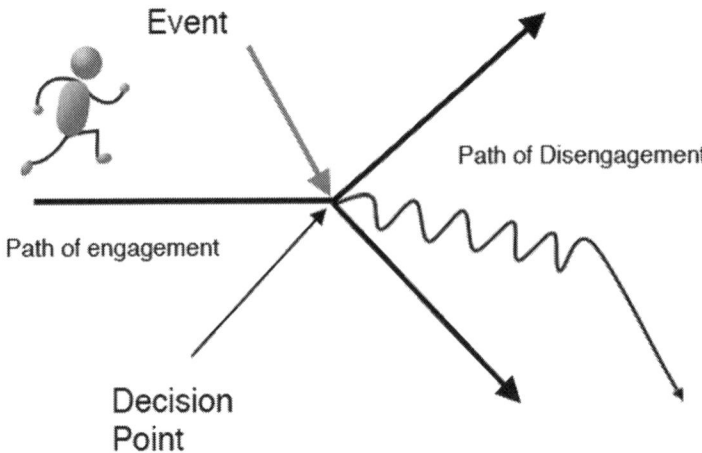

The path of disengagement is very familiar to all of us. It is a well-trodden path and sadly very popular. When events arrive and we don't respond to them, we step off the Path of Engagement. At first it's very subtle and we barely notice it. Later it becomes more pronounced and problematic.

What happens, is that all those wonderful feelings we had when we were in a state of engagement start to wear off. The first things to start to fade, just a bit, are your energy and your gratitude. As more events turn up which we don't respond to, the further we go down the path and the more those feelings start to wear off. (figure 5)

Great energy
Gratitude
Excited
Positive
Enthusiastic
Optimistic
Happy
Interested
Curious
Focused
Generous
Kind
Collaborative
Proud
Confident

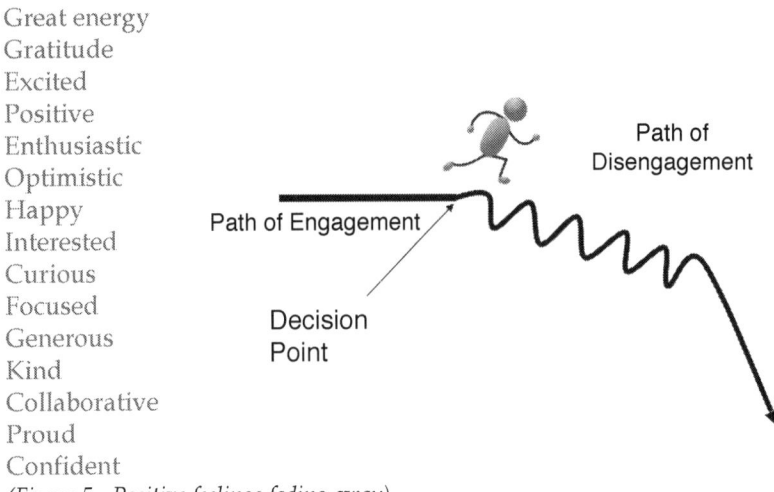

(Figure 5 - Positive feelings fading away)

When I was fully on the path of engagement and I was asked 'How's it going with Sylvie?' I would respond straight away with 'I must be the luckiest man in the world, this is like a dream come true'. If I was asked about my new job I'd be just as positive. 'I'm really, really happy, this has been a great move for me....The culture's just right and I can see myself doing really well here, my boss is extremely supportive'.

As I enter the early stages of disengagement though, my tone changes a bit. It's not bad, just not quite as brilliant. 'No, no, it's good, it's good, you know....we're very happy'. Stay on the path of disengagement a bit longer and those feelings start to completely disappear. If you keep walking down that path, soon enough you will reach 'The Numb Point'. (Figure 6)

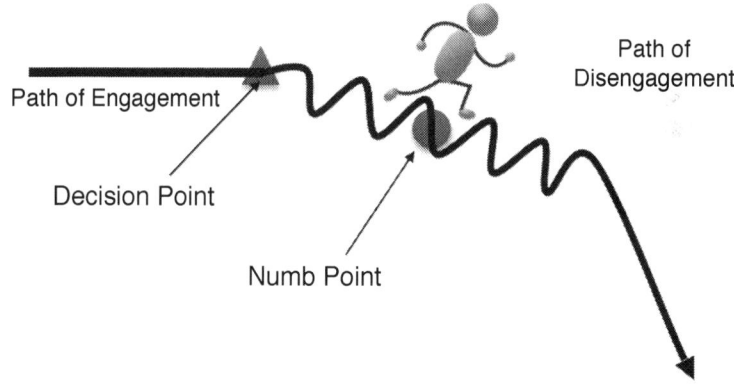

(Figure 6 - The Numb Point)

The Numb Point is just that. I don't feel good, I don't feel bad, I just feel, well, nothing really.

The new CEO turns up at our office and he's getting all excited about his new programme. 'So are we up for it, are you willing to give this 100%!!' she exhorts. Yeah....whatever... is about all I can muster up. I just don't have it in me anymore to get all excited about something. I've seen it all before. I just don't feel it, even if I'd quite like to. I don't really feel I'm going anywhere, I would love to have a sense of purpose, but I just don't. I watch a lot of TV and Facebook gets a lot of attention. Those positive feelings have gone and everything feels a bit repetitive. Days come and go. Have you ever been to the numb point? Can you think of people that are there now? Have you ever presented to a room full of numb people? Frightening isn't it!

Faking it
The more politically astute have already worked out that even if you don't feel it, it's important to pretend. Pretence is particularly important when; senior people are around, it's appraisal time, you want promotion or other similar opportunities may come your way. This often takes the form of:
- Outwardly agreeing with ideas you actually think aren't that good
- Pretending you like the boss (if you don't)
- Looking particularly busy when the boss is around and chilling out when they are not (you know that look....the 'I've never seen anything quite so interesting on my screen look').

As a leader or manager, this is quite tricky. Some people have what I call 'advanced sucking-up skills' and sometimes it's hard to tell who is really on the path and who isn't. The real problem is that whilst everyone may look like they agree with you and they all look hard at it, productivity is down, customer service is degrading and complaints are up. Hmmm.

If I've hit the Numb Point and a friend asks me how it's going with Sylvie, I might say 'It's OK, we're working at it...you know how it is'.

Before we go any further, let me clarify my view on a couple of things and take stock:

1. I don't know anyone who can remain totally on the Path of Engagement forever. This would require sainthood or chemicals. That would be rather odd. In reality, we oscillate. Sometimes, I'm fully on the path and sometimes events turn up and I may take a brief trip down the early stages of disengagement. The trick is to make sure you don't spend too long down there and make your way back when you notice you've slipped. Ideally, you want to move between feeling fully positive most of the time, with the occasional dip into OK-land. Anything up until the Numb point is ok. At least you are still feeling some of the positives. That's not a bad thing.
2. If you are managing someone, or a colleague in your team starts to slip down the slippery slope, they are relatively easy to bring back early on. Speed is of the essence. You don't want to leave this for too long as it becomes a habit, a worsening habit. It's the same for partners and friends.

Opposition

If you go beyond the Numb point, then something very different happens. The Opposites of those positive feelings start to turn up. (figure 7) Have a look at the list below. Sound familiar?

I was feeling	I'm now feeling
Great energy	Lethargic and tired all the time
Gratitude	I'm owed, where's mine
Excited	Bored
Positive	Cynical
Enthusiastic	Moaning and complaining
Optimistic	Pessimistic
Happy	Sad
Interested	Couldn't care less
Curious	Opinionated
Focused	Distracted
Generous	Counting and comparing
Helpful	Unobliging, blocking
Bright	Dull
Proud	Embarrassed
Confident	Doubtful
ENGAGED	DISENGAGED

The first two that start to go, as we mentioned before, are often your energy and your gratitude. Beyond the Numb Point, I start to feel tired a lot and sometimes even find it hard to stay awake in the afternoon. Suddenly, Fridays become important landmarks and Mondays begin to hold great dread. I'm no longer grateful, I feel owed. Where's my bonus? Where's my pay increase?

Before I was grateful. Now I'm counting and comparing. In the beginning, I was making Sylvie cups of tea just because I thought she'd love it. Now, I'm counting, how many breakfasts I've made, how many breakfasts she's made, how many times I made the bed, how many times she's emptied the dish washer.

At work, I'm now very sensitive and interested in who get's what and why. I'm counting and comparing. How come that department gets that and we only get this….how come I've been here for ten years and a new person can walk in off the street and get that? It's not fair, it's not right. Not only do I have opinions, I'm right about them. It's not me, it's them!

When you go beyond the Numb Point, cynicism takes hold and your positively engaged colleagues start to look different. They don't just look engaged anymore, they are now 'Goody-Goodies, Shoe-lickers, Suckers and Losers'. Of course I don't realize this at the time, I just think 'I'm right!'.

As I get closer to the final State of Disengagement, not only are events turning up, I'm also manufacturing them. I turn small things into big things and twist innocent situations into personal insults, deliberately directed at me. I am proactively looking for things to moan and complain about. The opposites put me in a state of Opposition.

When I was positively engaged, I was very much in the 'Us' frame of mind. I wanted to be part of something great and all I wanted to do was contribute. Now, I am firmly in the 'Us and Them' mind set, who gives a damn anyway and all I want to do is get out here. People right down this end of the path are often threatening to leave but rarely ever do. It's sometimes termed 'Quit and Stay'. Every month I take the money with one hand and talk it down with the other.

Not only have I become cynical, I'm now the 'Captain of the Cynics Club'…and I'm on a recruitment drive. I'm particularly interested in new people and getting to them first, to show them the ropes before the 'suits' get to them. Imagine the scene. I'm around the back of the office having my cigarette and I'm talking to some new people. 'New aren't you…Yeah, I can tell.…You're smiling. They'll soon knock that out of you, I'm telling you!…You listen to me and I'll show you how to get on around here.…The one you've really got to watch out for is……..etc.'

If you remember, from the previous chapter, I was quoting from the Aon Hewitt Database global survey. This is what they had to say:

'Only 19% of people in work in Europe felt highly engaged. Disturbingly, an equal number, 19%, scored themselves as 'actively disengaged'. The report describes 'actively disengaged' as those employees who are 'actively destroying value through negativity'.

That's quite a significant number and will have a huge influence on a team, if it takes hold. If you choose to ignore it, or postpone engaging with it, it will have immediate negative consequences for your team, colleagues, customers and primarily yourself. Engaging with disengagement is a core skill of a good leader and a good friend for that matter.

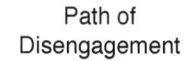

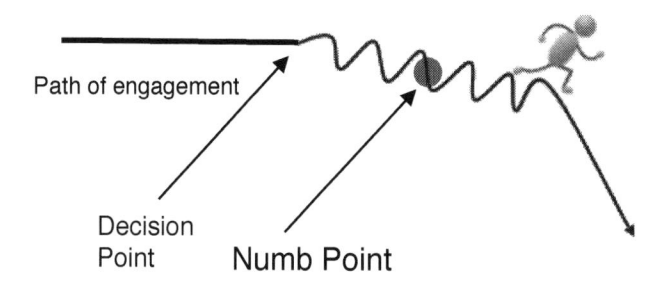

(Beyond the Numb Point - Opposition)

As you can probably tell we are getting close to the end game. Right at the end of this descent is a state called DRAMA

Drama

You weren't put on the planet to experience all this nasty stuff. You are actually meant to be enjoying it, so you may find yourself being delivered a DRAMA. (Figure 8)

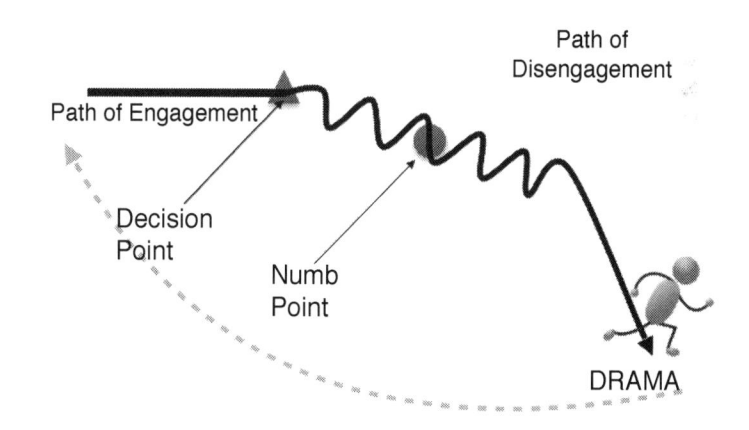

(Figure 8 - Drama)

Dramas can take many forms, but either way, they are painful and often protracted. Dramas can take months or even years to finally come to a head. In personal relationships, because you've been so negative, so prone to moaning and complaining and have been such a general pain in the you-know-what for so long, you may get dumped! At work, the business may be so tired of your negativity or low productivity that you may get invited to leave, despite the legal risk they may expose themselves to in the process of your removal.

Being down at the far end of disengagement is particularly bad for your health and you may get delivered a physical or health drama. Extreme disengagement comes with significant negative emotions such as anger, deep frustration and stress. These are well known triggers for some pretty nasty stress-related illnesses.

As well as being intense and rather painful experiences, the upside is that they are also strangely magical and somewhat miraculous. Those of you who have had dramas in their lives will know what I'm talking about.

Dramas have the ability to take you out of the game, but then maybe months, possibly years later, they drop you back on a new path, right at the beginning again and you get to have another go. (see the dotted grey line in figure 8). Hopefully you get it right this time around. Have you heard anyone say 'Do you know what, it was terrible at the time, but if all that hadn't of happened, I never would have met you….Can I get you a cup of tea xxx'

The Full Model

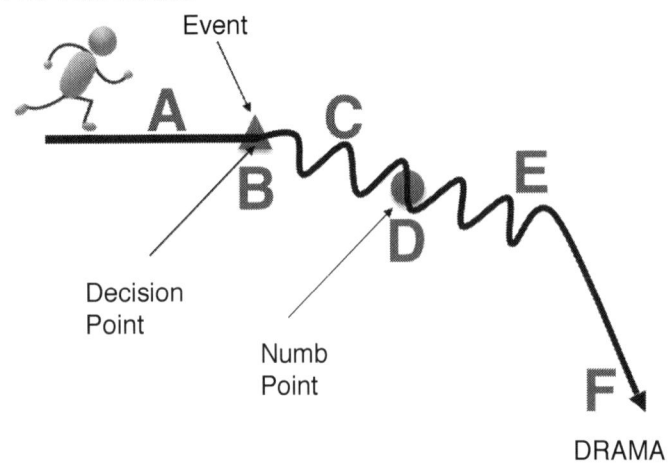

Event

A
B C
   D E

Decision Point

Numb Point

F

DRAMA

There we, have, it, the full model of the 'States of Engagement'. Let's take stock before we continue.

1. This descent is not inevitable. Many people are able to keep themselves on the Path of Engagement and reverse as soon as they feel themselves going down the slippery path.
2. The further down the path you go, the harder it is to get back quite so easily. As human beings, we are very habit-forming. Moaning and complaining is a hard habit to shake off.
3. It's much better to catch yourself out in the early stages of disengagement and return to your original positivity, rather than take the 'dramatic' route back to a new path. It's very painful and can last a very long time.
4. People that are close to, or are now in the 'Drama' State become somewhat 'dramatic' themselves. This is particularly noticeable in someone's word selection. For example: an accurate statement could be 'sometimes you don't empty the dishwasher'. The dramatic version would be 'You never empty the dishwasher!' There is a tendency to use what the linguists call Universal Quantifiers, words such as: never, always, every time.

Let's pause for a minute and have a closer look at your own situation. On the previous page, I have outlined the full engagement model and have labelled each State with a letter. I have also summarized the primary Emotions of Engagement and have provided some examples of common Events (on the following page) that tend to trigger decision points.

Spend a few moments to consider your own state of engagement. This may differ between work, home, friendships and activities. For example, you may feel disengaged at work, but feel fully engaged with your buddies in the football team. I suggest you initially go for work and home. During any day, you may also experience the full range of emotions. What we are looking for is your usual or most frequent state, as opposed to your peaks and troughs.

The States of Engagement

- A Fully Engaged
- B Events are hitting
- C Positives wearing off
- D Numb Point
- E The Opposites
- F Drama

The Emotions of Engagement

Fully Engaged	**Disengaged**
Great energy	Lethargic and tired all the time
Gratitude	I'm owed, where's mine
Excited	Bored
Positive	Cynical
Enthusiastic	Moaning and complaining
Optimistic	Pessimistic
Happy	Sad
Interested	Couldn't care less
Curious	Opinionated
Focused	Distracted
Generous	Counting and comparing
Helpful	Unobliging, blocking
Bright	Dull
Proud	Embarrassed
Confident	Doubtful

Typical negative Events

Broken promises
A disengaged boss
Communication and decisions that show a lack of trust or respect
A lack of events such as thanks, appreciation, recognition
Too much change without the time to embed any of it
A show of disinterest in the things that are most important to people; their kids, partners, hobbies
Poorly communicated changes
Favouritism (conscious or unconscious)
You get asked for your opinions and then management do the opposite of what you suggested
A lack of investment and using people's good will
Unfairness or irregularities in remuneration and reward
Retraction of benefits
Changes in working hours or shift patterns, without proper consultation or care
Unjustified or unexplained promotions
Politics
Being taken for granted
A lack of consideration
Slow/no decision-making ('I'm looking into it; I'll get back to you')

This is not an exhaustive list, but it certainly covers some of the major culprits. I'm sure you could add many more! There are an awful lot of them! Let me ask you a few simple questions, so you can complete the table I've created for you over the page. This will provide you with an opportunity to examine your current level of engagement and evaluate where improvements can be made.

Notes on completing your own analysis
If you don't have a team, think of the people you work with most closely. Who are your major stake holders for example?
- Under the heading 'State', use the simple category of A, B, C, D, E or F, referring to the States of Engagement in the Full Model, as laid out on the previous page.
- Under the heading Indicators and Symptoms, write down the main things you are observing which makes you think someone is an, A, B, C, D, E or F.
- Under the section; Your Boss, I have left space for up to three people. In todays highly matrixed management, many people have a number of reporting lines. If you've just got one, that's fine, just do one entry for that section.
- Under the section; Myself, I have left a bit more space for you to explore your own indicators and symptoms a little further. It may also be useful to add a few of the Events you experienced (positive or negative), that may have contributed to your assessment of your current State of Engagement.

In reality, people move up and down these States all the time. You can even make a whole round trip in a day, or even an hour!! I'm sure we've all done that. I'm interested in your average state, where do you and your team hang out most? What is the average habitual state?

If you wish, grab a sheet of paper and make your own private list.

Enjoy!

My Team
A - Fully engaged, B - Events are hitting, C - Positives wearing off, D - Numb, E - Opposites, F - Drama

NAME	LEVEL	INDICATORS AND SYMPTOMS

Your Boss
A - Fully engaged, B - Events are hitting, C - Positives wearing off, D - Numb, E - Opposites, F - Drama

NAME	LEVEL	INDICATORS AND SYMPTOMS

Myself

NAME	LEVEL	INDICATORS AND SYMPTOMS

Teams and Engagement

The States of Engagement
A   Fully Engaged
B   Events are hitting
C   Positives wearing off
D   Numb Point
E   The opposites
F   Drama

The team you inherit, take over or create, will usually have differing levels of individual engagement contained within it. The mix will determine your approach to building a brilliant team.

Below, I have outlined some of the typical combinations you may experience and some of the archetypal themes and features you are likely to encounter. The engagement spectrum is broad, so I have selected three points on that spectrum and highlighted how team characteristics change, depending on the varying levels of engagement. Both ends of the spectrum are extremes, but in reality, not all that uncommon. Quickly glance over each team type and in the 'Engagement Spectrum' diagram on the next page, identify where you think your own team is best represented. (Figure 10)

The Ideal Team - All members of the team are either A or B
- There is a strong desire to perform and contribute
- There is a willingness to go beyond the minimum required
- Creativity and innovation is free-flowing
- Trust and honesty is clearly present
- Full empowerment is possible with minimal oversight
- There is a solution orientation to obstacles and problems.
- Rapport is based on sharing a common purpose
- Ownership and taking responsibility are high
- Disagreement is contained within alignment to objectives
- Pro-active willingness to celebrate each other
- Negative feedback is viewed as constructive and useful
- Feedback and suggestions are readily accepted
- Poor standards are usually addressed at peer level
- Mistakes are openly and immediately admitted
- Meetings are focused and flow well. Phones are off.
- Negative comments are taken directly to the person concerned
- Moaning is off the menu
- Positive attrition (the people you prefer to move on, do)

The OK Team - There are a mix of A, B, C, D and an E
- There is a mixed willingness to perform. Some need pushing.
- Generally, people work hard, but few enjoy going that extra mile
- Creativity and innovation only comes from a couple of people, some don't seem that interested
- A willingness to trust more, but productivity takes quite a dip when the manager is not present
- Reluctance to empower, as self-motivation is so varied
- Solutions to problems are often provided by the manager
- Rapport is mixed, based on who gets on with who; danger of the manager having favourites
- Little ownership and responsibility; delegation limited to better performers
- We avoid disagreement, as it seems to lower performance
- Some people don't get involved with celebration, so it's done more on an individual basis
- Negative feedback is often seen as bad news; some feedback is therefore not given
- Some feedback is accepted with reluctance
- The manager is the primary person who addresses poor performance or standards
- Mistakes take time to reveal themselves; lots of 'reasons' for why performance is low
- Taking responsibility for outcomes and results is not a popular idea
- It's hard to get the energy up in some meetings; always the same people contributing
- Talking behind people's back is quite common
- Moaning is frequent and relatively habitual

The Nightmare Team - An A or B, mainly C, D, E and an F or two
- After a while, good performers get dragged down
- More desire to complain than perform; some in open opposition
- Creativity is negatively channeled into blame or explaining why things can't be done
- Open distrust; there is suspicion between staff and management
- Empowerment is not an option; some staff need close oversight
- No solutions to problems, just problems. 'It can't be done and this is why'.
- Rapport is based on having a common enemy; we all agree the boss is useless!
- Victim stance often adopted 'If I had the tools, the salary, the time I could...'

- People disagree without being open to alternatives; some passive aggressive behaviour
- Celebration or thanks is met with cynicism or suspicion; 'It's a bit late for that now!'
- Constructive feedback is viewed as an insult, a put-down or a black mark
- Feedback and suggestions are sometimes rejected or disputed
- Peer feedback about poor standards would not be accepted. 'Who do you think you are?'
- Mistakes are sometimes concealed or high levels of blame and innocence are proclaimed
- Meetings are often adversarial, interrupted or even hijacked; high in-meeting phone usage.
- Positive people stay quiet and start looking for alternatives
- Gossip and negative banter is the common language; positivity is met with cynicism
- Moaning is the primary currency

The Engagement Spectrum
Where is your team? Draw an imaginary needle on the dial.

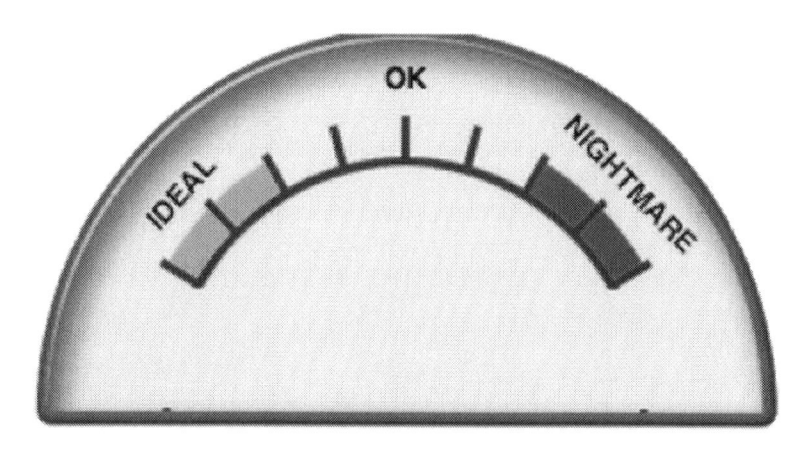

(Figure 10 - The Engagement Spectrum)

Now that we are looking at teams from an engagement perspective, we can start to see how engagement has such an impact on the team or company results. Let's have a quick reminder of what organisations are achieving who occupy the upper quartile of engagement.

AREA	TOP QUARTILE AGAINST BOTTOM QUARTILE
Profit	x 2
Revenue	x 2.5
Innovation	59%
Productivity	18%
Employee turnover	down 40%
Customer advocacy	12%

Before we turn our minds to how we can use this understanding to transform, improve or refine our own situations, there are a few other considerations to explore.

A - Fully engaged, B - Events are hitting, C - Positives wearing off, D - Numb, E - Opposites, F- Drama

What do you imagine typically happens to someone who is an A if they find themselves in a team that is predominantly D or beyond? There are a number of options:
- They leave as they realize this is not the place for them
- After a while, they feel stupid or naive for putting in 100%
- Everyone else seems to be coasting and getting the same remuneration or treatment
- Performance drops a couple of gears
- A's feel ostracized and retract, as they are not part of 'the gang'

What happens if the team is predominantly A - C with an E or two (Opposites) and the manager is not tackling the situation?
- Respect for the manager drops
- Overall standards start to fall away
- The manager may also be seen to be pandering or giving special attention to the person in opposition, they dodge the real issues and let trouble-makers get away with it
- The manager may dilute their messages to avoid disapproval, reducing their ability to inspire and lead

- The manager, unwilling to leave their comfort zone, changes what they say and how they say it, depending who they are taking to.
- The team don't get a clear single message.

What happens if your boss is a D,E or beyond?
- It's very hard to stay motivated
- After a while, there is no point coming up with improvements, as it's always met with; 'reasons why it might not work', 'it's been tried before' or 'we're already looking into that'
- People have a natural desire to be appreciated by their boss, so you may find yourself outwardly agreeing with them, whereas in truth you have an alternative view. This desire significantly degrades your self-esteem. To a great extent, self-esteem is at its highest when your beliefs, values and actions overlap. This type of behaviour drives self-esteem in the opposite direction and will impact your energy and self-respect
- You may find yourself on the end of unreasonable workloads, feeling intimidated, or unable to talk about it for fear of consequences
- Disagreement does not appear to be an option
- A manager may appear unavailable for communication, be that for feedback or personal motivation.
- It probably won't be long before you are numb and repeating your woes to your poor partner!

What happens if your boss is an A, with the occasional dip into B?

Well, that's the good stuff and under those conditions you may get to find out just how good you can be.

I know from experience, the difference between having a boss that is an A, rather than something further down the slope. It's quite life-changing, literally. My advice would be: don't leave this down to luck. Where you can, get a boss that is fully-engaged; if you think about it, the alternative really shouldn't be considered. Whilst it may seem very daunting at the time, do all you can to avoid having a manager that is well down the disengagement route. You deserve better than that.

Growing up with a dad that regularly makes mum cups of tea, just because he thought she'd love it, is a very different lesson to witnessing a man when asked 'ohh I'd love a cup of tea' replies with

'Why don't you make it yourself'. How good is your 'random acts of tea making' these days?

'It's one thing having mentors, but are you willing to be one?' That is a good question and one we will delve into further.

Staying engaged, even when difficult events are flying about, is a choice. I'm often amazed by people that hit tragedy in their lives but choose to remain positive. Some even use the experience to renew themselves and launch a whole new chapter in their life. They remind me of a simple principle, 'You always have a choice'.

The Spirit of Engagement

Labels everywhere

Change starts with the person sat in the chair you are sitting in. How engaged are you? From what has been discussed so far, I think it's pretty clear that you can't expect your team to be A's and B's, unless you are traveling that road yourself.

I meet many managers that tell me 'If only I had a better team', 'Why can't they be like my last team' or 'If only that person wasn't in my team'.

I find a useful principle to adopt is :

> YOUR TEAM ARE A REFLECTION OF YOU

This is arguably not necessarily true on your first day, or by the end of the first week. However, a month or two in, I certainly stand by this statement.

Consider this. If you have someone in your team that is in opposition, an E, that in itself going to be an event for you; if you are not careful, you may find yourself going down the slippery slope in relationship to them. You may even find yourself giving them a label and sticking an invisible Post-It note on their forehead... 'The difficult one'. The trouble is with labels, people become them.

I'm sure it's happened to you. I tend to be more intelligent around the people that think I'm intelligent, I'm more goofy around the people that think I'm goofy, I'm funnier around the people that think I'm funny. I'm more loving around those people that think I'm loving. I tend to seek out those people that give me positive labels. I call them friends.

I once had a boss called Bert. He was a very tall and an annoyingly handsome Dutch guy. Despite that flaw, he was without doubt the best boss I've ever had. He had a fantastic ability to give people positive labels and then talk to them as if they were that. My label read something like this:

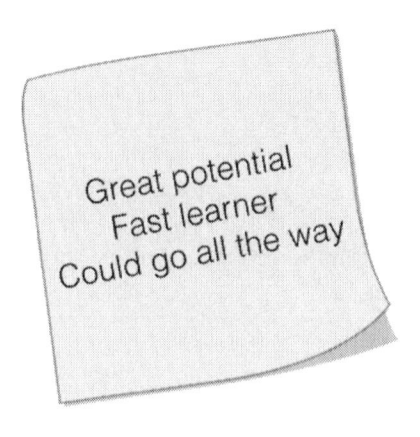

> Great potential
> Fast learner
> Could go all the way

I was only with Bert for a year. I joined him as a manager of a major international business and left as a director. That would not have happened without that man's tutelage, direction and guidance. He shone a light on me that was brighter than the one I even shone on myself. He saw great potential in me, he thought I was a fast learner, he felt I had a good heart and somehow knew I had it in me to go all the way. I became a direct reflection of what he chose to see in me.

To be honest, although I'd never admit it, I thought I was his favourite. It was only when I was at my leaving party and was having farewell drinks with my colleagues, that it came out that we all thought we were his favourites, he was that good. Thanks Bert, you are a diamond! I've also had the misfortune to have had one or two bosses that have given me quite different labels. Guess what, without realizing it, I started to become those labels too.

> Medium talent
> Nothing special
> No promotion yet

Opportunities or challenges didn't come my way, I was talked to differently than some of the others, I didn't feel special in any way and found it hard to really push myself. Again, I started conforming to the invisible labels I sensed were being attached to me.

This labelling concept is actually quite a powerful and causative factor. When I speak to most people about it, we all realize just how many labels there are flying about. Do you have labels for the members of your team? Do you have a label or two for your boss? Do you have labels for other departments, or even for customers. Do you think customers might have some labels for you or your business? Some of these labels will be good, some not so.

In my experience, customers get their labels out within a few seconds of interacting with your service, be that on the telephone, in a shop or even on-line. Quite often, the labels they give are in reaction to the label they feel that have just been given. Most of the labels I give people are in response to the labels I believe they have given me....It tends to work that way around.

This has huge implications for engagement. The more engaged I am, the more likely I am to view people and customers positively and therefore the quality of the labels I am likely to afford people. The less engaged I am, the poorer the quality of label I dish out. Sound familiar?

In my own business, many companies I speak to are on some kind of journey. Some are currently calling that journey 'Going from good to great'. That's a noble journey to go on. If you are serious about that journey, you will want to get serious about how you manage disengagement. 'OK' companies have OK standards when it comes to disengagement. It's tolerated to various degrees, but nevertheless tolerated.

One of the things I have noticed about great teams, is that they have a minimum standard when it comes to disengagement. The minimum standard is NONE. It is absolutely not an option. Great teams draw a line. That doesn't mean getting the axe out immediately, far from it. What it does mean, is deciding to take a stance and helping people to either make the journey back to engagement or find another game somewhere else. In my experience, people actually prefer being engaged, despite what it looks like from the outside. What's needed is someone willing to believe in them and apply a bit of tough love where required. Are you willing to get involved? Are you willing to roll up your sleeves and get down in the mud? Are you willing to leave your comfort zone, go beyond your labels and opinions and connect?

The easiest thing is to disengage from disengaged people, have opinions, give them labels and moan about them behind their back. There lies part of the problem. Your own disengagement causes the opposite of what you want.

In the first chapter, we mentioned IQ and EQ. When it comes to engagement, EQ is far more Important than IQ. This is particularly true when faced with disengagement. What helps is courage and compassion, what doesn't is opinions and excuses. Great teams push themselves to have the tricky conversations about engagement, lesser teams shy away.

If someone has gone numb or into opposition, stretch out your hand and talk about it. They'll always thank you for it afterwards, even the hard cases, so will your team! Some people however, are just not ready to give up their opposition. Inaction will have significant consequences. Bite the bullet and do what's right. You will be judged by how you deal with disengagement. Choose to be a leader. I don't mean get all alpha male and confront disengagement. Quite the opposite, engaging with disengagement means finding out what happened, what events led up to this and offering a path back.

The first step, of course, in any journey like this relates directly back to the first sentence of this chapter. How engaged are YOU?

As a leader, people manager or perhaps most importantly, as a partner, it is critical to manage our own genuine level of engagement and to stay as far to the left as possible. I am a big fan of Simon Sinek. Amongst other things, he has produced some wonderful TED Talks and videos; 'How great leaders inspire action' and 'Leaders eat last' particularly come to mind. One of his signature statements is:

'Leaders are called leaders because they go first.' Nowhere is this more important than when it comes to engagement.

I jokingly tell people that 'It's not written in your contract of employment, but if you spread a little lemon juice on it and heat it over a candle, you will see a clause written in invisible ink'.

1.1 I promise to stay engaged.

Where the game is won and lost

Being deeply social creatures, much of our engagement is influenced by communication, or the lack of it. Communication, as we know, is not just about the words we use. Most of us are now very familiar with these concepts. There's a lot more to it than that.

Communication happens on many, many levels. You will probably have read books, attended lectures and participated in workshops on the subject, examining many of the fascinating layers and aspects involved.

Most of what gets taught in work-related training sessions and study groups, refers to the more common aspects of communication; What to say and how to say it. This is particularly so for people in management and customer-facing areas. There are far more powerful forces at play in communication, and these other dimensions really are where the game is won or lost. Let me walk you through a brief hierarchy of communication and I will explain what I mean.

We'll start with Words, the first level of the SPHERES of INFLUENCE

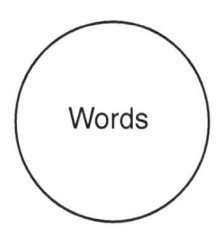

(Words)

If I was to say to you, in a straightforward way, 'That's a nice haircut'. You would probably reply 'Thank you' or something else to that effect, as you imagine I was paying you a compliment.

Now let's say I was to say exactly the same words to you, but change my tone to one of sarcasm, accompanied by a look of derision on my face, then you would take it quite differently. This would now seem to be an insult and your response would be quite the opposite. I used the same words, but you believe I am now saying something completely different; the opposite in fact. We are all familiar with this and know a good deal about vocal tone, body language and facial expressions.

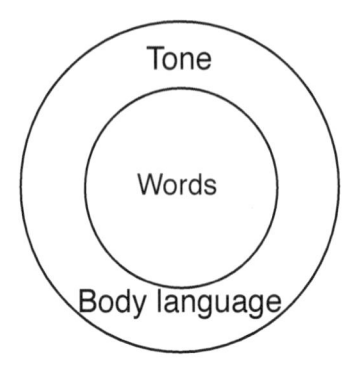

As human beings, we can't help it. If the tone and body language are saying one thing and the words another, we always believe the tone and the non-verbal signals. It's the way we are wired up. The neocortex understands the words and what they mean perfectly well, but the more powerful limbic brain, whilst having no capacity for language or logic, decides exactly what it means. It bases its understanding on the more trustworthy source of vocal tones, facial expressions and body language.

The scientists tell us that our physiology (vocal tones, facial expressions and body language, plus a few other bits like breathing rate and depth, skin tone and muscle tension) communicates about 93% of our total message. That's a lot! *(figure 11)*

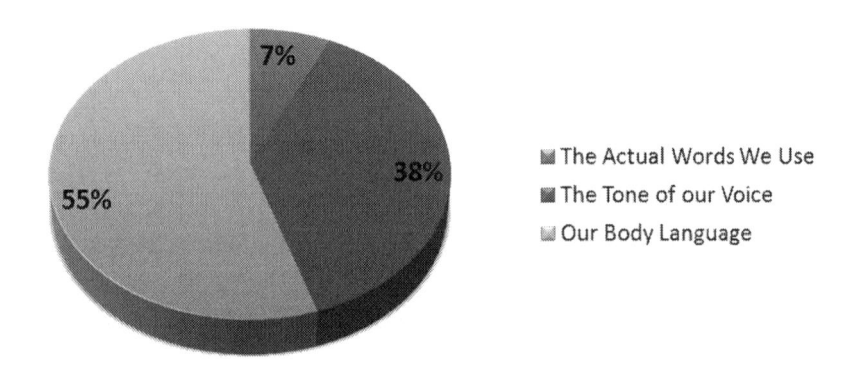

(Figure 11 - Words, tone and body language)

When we prepare for important meetings, difficult conversations, presentations or indeed speeches, we naturally tend to gravitate to 'what to say?' and 'how should I say it?'.

I'd like to suggest that there are two additional spheres, that are significantly more influential than words, or even our tone, body language or facial expressions. These two larger spheres exert far greater bearing over what someone believes you really mean and profoundly determine the level to which someone will be willing to listen, consider and respond to what you are communicating.

For me, it was quite a revelation when I was introduced to the two larger outer 'Spheres of Influence'. Prior to this, I didn't realize these were skill areas I could learn and assimilate. I saw them much more as a matter of luck, genes or parental upbringing. Some people just seemed to have the gift of the gab, a way with words or a magnetic personality.

Communication is central to our ability to achieve and enjoy so many things. Improvements in this area are worth their weight in gold, especially when it comes to transforming engagement.

As one of my favourite poets, Khalil Gibran said:

> *'Between what is said*
> *and not meant,*
> *and what is meant but not said,*
> *most of love is lost'*

Let's spend some time exploring the two outer 'spheres of influence' and the powerful role they play, in and out of work. They speak directly to our emotional centres and shape how we feel, form judgements and make decisions. Time invested here will reap great reward.

Rapport

The next and increasingly more powerful Sphere of Influence is rapport.

```
        RAPPORT
          Tone
         Words
       Body language
```

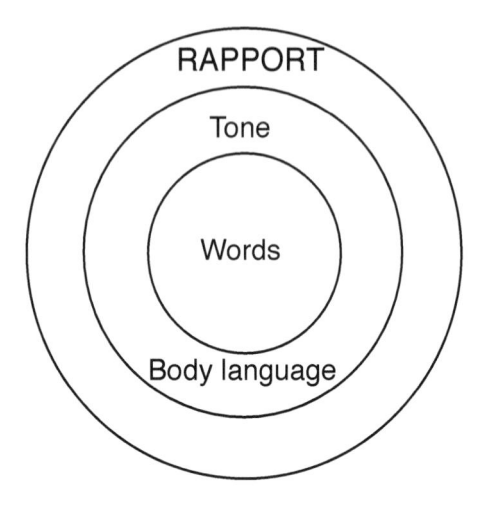

(Figure 12 - Rapport)

There is much to say about rapport. Wikipedia defines rapport as follows:

Rapport is a close and harmonious relationship in which the people or groups concerned understand each other's feelings or ideas and communicate well.

The word stems from the old French verb *rapporter* which literally means to carry something back and, in the sense of how people relate to each other means that **what one person sends out the other sends back**. For example, they may realize that they share similar values, beliefs, knowledge, or politics, music or sports.

Rapport is very powerful and like vocal tones, facial expressions and body language, it changes what someone thinks is really being said, at an even deeper level.

Let's keep our haircut example going...

Let's say you and I had known each other for years, way before we joined the company we now work at. We are the best of friends and really hit it off. Imagine we joined on the same day and went through the same induction programme together. It soon becomes very clear to everyone that we are very good friends indeed; whenever we are in the same room, everyone knows there is going to be a lot of laughter, fun and positive humour. Got the scene?

One day, out of the blue, I come up to you and say 'That's a nice haircut' but with the same sarcastic tone, accompanied by a look of derision on my face, as in the previous example. What would you think I was really saying or trying to do? Since our rapport was so strong, you'd immediately know I was just having a laugh and poking fun. You wouldn't even have to think twice about it, you'd know it instantly at a gut-level (limbic level). In fact, you would probably say something equally sarcastic back to me 'Well, at least I've got some!' I would laugh deeply at your retort, even though you were mocking me.

Let's say the opposite was the case. Suppose you and I didn't like each other, in fact, didn't like each other at all. Imagine we had recently had a number of heated public run-ins and had to be cautioned about it. We have no rapport at all. One day, out of the blue, I come up to you and say 'That's a nice haircut', but with the same sarcastic tone, accompanied by a look of derision on my face, as in the previous example. What would you think I was really saying? I don't think it requires too much imagination to work out that this is not going to end well, for either of us.

Isn't that interesting? In both cases, exactly the same was said and yet the outcome could not be more polarized. Rapport, or the lack of it, is highly influential in terms of what inferences or meaning people take from a communication. It entirely governs the state of the relationship and alters the context through which someone chooses to understand what is being said. Here is another example I'm sure you can resonate with.

This example is broken into two scenes.

Scene 1. The context is: 'I have a great rapport with my boss'.

Let's say I'm making a presentation to a number of my colleagues. The room is quite large and as is often the case, the main wall facing into the rest of the office is made of glass. My boss walks past, glances at me, looks irritated and continues to walk to her office. As our rapport is very good, I assume something has upset her and I decide to drop in at lunchtime to make sure she is okay.

Scene 2. The context is: 'I have a poor rapport with my boss'.

I'm making a presentation to a number of my colleagues in the same room as before. My boss walks past, glances at me, looks irritated and continues to walk to her office. As the rapport is poor, I automatically assume I've done something wrong, or in some way I am in trouble. My strategy is HIDE!!

'Rapport, or the lack of it, changes what I think things mean and significantly influences my behaviour. This in turn creates virtuous or vicious, self-reinforcing circles.'

Rapport trumps words, tone and body language, every time.

Have you ever listened to or been involved in a complaint where a good rapport has been established right from the outset. You are highly likely to observe 'big issues becoming small issues' and a resolution, or at least a path to a resolution revealing itself, as if by magic. Conversely, where there is no rapport, small things become big things. The smallest of things irritate and become showstoppers. It's almost as if the person complaining is proactively looking for things to be unhappy about. As the complainant, I want you to really understand just how unhappy I am, I may even exaggerate what I'm complaining about and the size of the problem it is causing me. For example, 'I've been waiting for ten minutes' (It was actually three minutes, twenty three seconds). 'I had to take the whole day off to deal with this' (I had the day off anyway) etc. Ever done anything like that?

Rapport drives the state of engagement between people and you can particularly see it in complaint situations.

Think back to the Path of Engagement model. Where there is no or little rapport, there is a strong tendency for the person complaining to take up a position well down the Path of Disengagement. They go into direct opposition. You can hear it in their word choice and tone. Their language migrates towards the dramatic and they may unconsciously exaggerate the situation. The poor person on the other end of the phone is going to have a hard time. Once a conversation degrades in this fashion, there is not a lot of point focussing on saying sorry with a perfect tone (although that will help). The best course of action would be to pull hard on the rapport lever. On the other side of the equation, I've even heard quite a few phone calls where the customer services agent (let's say they are new) really messed up the call in terms of accuracy, resolution and content, but, because the rapport was good, it all ended up in a good place. Again, the reason for that is when a good level of rapport is established, both parties position themselves firmly on the left hand side of the Path of Engagement and go into direct co-operation and a state of helpfulness.

Mirrors all the way down

In the previous chapter, we looked at the principle of 'Your team is a reflection of you'. This is particularly true when it comes to rapport.

The level of rapport that exists between the people within an organisation is directly reflected in the level of rapport customers experience with that organisation.

'What is on the inside, flows to the outside'

I do remember laughing when I once overheard from around a corner, a particularly sincere but overly serious manager. He was 'ordering' his team to have more rapport with their customers. The downtrodden, numb looks on the team's faces told the real story. To be fair, I knew this guy quite well and he's a lovely man. He'd just got very inspired about the idea of rapport and was slightly overzealous in how he was communicating about it. However, it does prove one of the laws of rapport and many other things for that matter:

'Be it, to have it'

As my great friend Woody would say 'The only thing that is missing from any situation is the bit you're not putting in'.

Particularly at senior levels within an organisation, where there is no rapport, there are politics. Most people hate organisational politics. It serves as one of the primary triggers for causing Events for people.

Organisations with a lot of politics or power gaming at a senior level, provokes disengagement and subsequently suppresses the organisations' potential. Sometimes the skills and qualities that get you to the top of an organisation are not necessarily the ones you need once you get up there. Reducing politics at a senior level and replacing it with a healthier diet of rapport can be tricky. It sometimes involves strong characters who may have little appetite for this type of discussion. Again, this is potentially an 'out of the comfort zone' conversation' which your Limbic brain will try to steer you clear of. However, the effort will be handsomely repaid, with better engagement throughout and the possibility of some of the material improvements we looked at in the chapter 'Why get engaged?"

At a limbic level, rapport is experienced as the powerful emotions of trust and belonging, it's almost tribal. This is why I can call my brother a fool, but if you try and say the same thing to him, that's a completely different matter, more fool you!

It's these deep-seated feelings of **trust and belonging** that allows rapport to trump words, tone, facial expression and body language every time.

Rapport - Superficial to deep

Rapport happens at a number of levels, sometimes it can take the form of superficial exchanges based on pleasantries and general politeness, sometimes it can represent a life-long bond of deep love and reciprocity.

Some people are naturally good at it and others not so. My Mum, for example, is a complete master of it. Whoever she meets instantly falls instantly in love with her. She is as easy with complete strangers as she is with close family. She can sweet-talk anyone into doing anything. She is by no means good at providing rational argument for people to do things, but she has an amazing gift for getting people to 'want' to do things. This is the power of rapport.

Part of creating rapport, is being willing to remove the labels we give people and replacing them with better ones. This is a powerful skill and a habit worth creating. As discussed earlier, our minds have a label production department deeply secreted within our limbic brain. It's part of our survival patterning and serves to determine friend or foe, insider or outsider. We can't stop it, but we can train it.

If I think back to my masterful boss, Bert, one of the things he was exceptionally good at, was giving people good labels. Bert knew at some level, that people live up to the labels they are given. Perhaps one or both of his parents showed him this through the way they encouraged him, we'll never know. What I do know is he, metaphorically speaking, shone a light on me that was far brighter than the one I even shone on myself. His view of what he thought I was capable of was far greater than what I thought I was capable of. As a result of how he chose to see me, I grew rapidly like a bamboo shoot, at an almost perceptible rate. Bamboos are the fastest-growing plants in the world. Certain species of bamboo can grow 91 cm (3 ft) within a 24-hour period, at a rate of almost 4 cm an hour (a growth around 1 mm every 40 seconds).

My point is: if you could grow people in your own business at bamboo speed, you'd be one happy farmer!

My Mum was similar to Bert, she had this wonderful gift of seeing the positive in people. Don't mistake this for naivety, she's anything but. People that meet her seem to feel at some level in their being that 'who I am is good enough' and 'I am seen for the great person I really am'. Naturally, they respond by loving her straight back. I'm sure you know or have met someone like that. For me, this encapsulates that definition of the word rapport and its root in the French word 'rapporter': 'to carry (or give) something back'. People give back what they feel they are being given.

We are all super-sensitive and designed to assess how we are being viewed and what labels we feel we are being given. This is one of the major preoccupations of our powerful limbic minds and one that plays a huge role in how much rapport we allow ourselves to have with people.

When I'd left home in my early twenties, my parents used to come around to our house for a meal from time to time. The conversations would always vary depending on what was happening at the time, however, we always knew one thing, and one thing for sure. We knew what Mum was going to say at the end of the meal. 'Do you know what darling, I think that's the nicest meal I've ever had.' She said this without fail at the end of every meal we cooked for her. I used to think she was a permanent liar (sorry Mum, I meant exaggerator) and we had a bit of a family joke about it.

I now see this differently. She's done this so consistently all her life, not just around meals, that I now believe this is how she sees the world. Those of us that have the good fortune to come into contact with her, all get the positive treatment and a bit of her magic rubs off on each of us. There are many unsung heroes like this. Those ridiculously positive and outrageously optimistic mums and dads, teachers or mentors, to name but a few, who really do make, in the words of Louis Armstrong, 'A wonderful world'.

One of the skills and indeed the art of rapport isn't what your are seeing, it's how you are seeing. How well are you seeing?... and I'm not talking about your eyesight!

Are you willing to see the positive and upgrade the labels you give people? Are you willing to upgrade the labels you give yourself?

I'm not saying Bert never gave me a bad label. There were definitely a few times when he gave me some pretty bad labels. What he was good at though, was as soon as he was unhappy about something, he'd communicate about it straight away. He never let something like that go, never stored it up for a later date or left a mood hanging over me. He'd talk about it straight away and then completely drop it. Before you knew it, the bad label had been peeled off my forehead and the great one was replaced. Brilliant, that's quite a skill.

The truth for me is I'm 55 and I'm still making myself up as I go along, I think we all are. I am not the finished article, I'm changing, maturing and growing. A part of my mind however, likes to think it knows people, it thinks it knows what they are really like. I now don't think that's true. How could I possibly know that? I'm still learning about myself! The moment you think you really know someone, that's the day you stop being curious. The truth is, I don't really know people, I'm just good at making labels up and thinking I know people.

Since I've started seeing things this way, I've noticed I can see a greater range of possibility and potential within people and find it easier to see the positive. At some level Bert seemed to know that and gave everyone the benefit of the doubt. He chose to see the highest in people. He grew a lot of very tall people.

Knowing the score

Imagine some friends and I got tickets to see an Arsenal vs Manchester United football match. It's late in the season and this is a crucial match. The outcome of this game could decide who lifts the cup in six weeks time.

My son also happened to have a football game in the morning, on the same day. His team had been doing well all season and are now in the final of their junior league championship. This is a 'Dad must attend event', no question. Non-attendance is not an option. I was excited to attend Harrison's match, but it did mean that I would probably miss the first half of the Arsenal game.

Naturally, I choose to attend both and sure enough, due to difficult traffic conditions, only managed to make the Arsenal game for the second half. Realizing I'm going to be late, I send a text to my friends as soon as I arrive at the stadium. They message back immediately, telling me exactly where they are and to hurry up as the second half is about to begin.

I run to the meeting point and see them straight away. What do you imagine is the very first thing I say to them? That's right. 'What's the score!!?' That's what anyone would ask.

Picture a scene where each of my friends look at each other in turn, shrug their shoulders and say 'I'm not sure' and ask the friend next to them 'You we're keeping the score, weren't you?'. 'No. I think I missed that bit', 'Oh well, it doesn't matter, it's only a game!'

Immediately, I would know they were just joking and soon enough, we'd all be laughing. Everyone in the stadium knows the score.

Why? Because they are interested. Very, very interested.

Not only do they know the score, they could tell you in great detail the precise sequence of passes that led up to the goal, how the defender got wrong footed and how the ref got it completely wrong!!

Why? Because they are interested, very interested. This is universally the same for any sport, be it baseball, tennis, rugby or any other. Where there is passion, there is deep interest.

Why am I labouring this point and what has rapport and engagement got to do with knowing the score?

I've been managed by some people and the truth is, they really weren't interested in me at all. How do I know? Simple. They don't even know the names of the people closest to me in my life; my wife and my son. They want me to have rapport with our customers. But they don't want to have rapport with me. They don't know me at all. They don't know anything about the things that really matter to me; My partner, my son, my parents, my hobbies, my passions. They don't even know the basics like what their names are!!

They are not interested. Not interested at all.

'Relationships start by giving' and like any relationship, the first thing to start giving is your attention and your interest.

I'm not saying managers have to take their team out for dinner once a week, or invite them around to their place every other weekend. What I am saying, is that you can't expect people to excel, to be interested and engaged and to have great rapport with customers, if their manager shows little outward interest in them. It's not a secret. People know if you're genuinely interested or not. It's one of those things you can't fake.

This is something our powerful limbic minds monitor all the time. Our acceptance within the tribe is core to our sense of well-being, participation and trust. We all have the capacity to sense it and feel it. Trust is not something that can be taken, it can only be given. Ignore it at your peril.

Let's do a quick 'know the score' audit and assess how well you know the people in your team and those that work around you.

If you don't score well, I'm not necessarily saying you don't care, but you may want to reassess to what degree that care is hidden and how you might want to turn the volume knob up in that area.

Without checking your personnel files, smart phones or anything like that, quickly complete the following simple table. If you don't know the answer, write 'don't know'. Please don't guess, if you are not sure, just write 'don't know'. Tell the truth, this is not a competition, this is just for your own purposes.

On a piece of paper, or on an excel spreadsheet if you are that way inclined, draw four simple columns with about twelve or so rows for each member of your team and your boss. Again, if you don't have a team, write the names of the people you work most closely with. At the top of each column write the headings: 'name , partner's name, children's names and hobbies or interests. Complete the table by filling in each member of your team under the columns you've just written.

How did you find it? Interesting? Congratulations if you could complete all of it. If not, take a mental note to put your attention on this area.

When I first did this, I was rather surprised how many 'don't knows' I entered in the boxes. It was a real wake up call for me. I genuinely thought I had a good rapport and had a lot of interest in the people in my team. When it really came down to it, I realized a simple thing. I was subconsciously more interested in their results, than I was in them. For me, this was an important lesson and one that changed me.

This also partly explained to me why so many people love my Mum. If you watch her, after a while, you start to notice where her attention is. It's totally on other people, her questions by their very nature convey interest and concern, she responds expressively to what people are saying and feeling. Is my mother nosey? No, she's just very interested in what you have to say.

Bert was a bit like that. I always got the sense he liked people. That's not to say he didn't pull me up from time to time, but underneath he liked me.

I'm a simple person. 'I like people that I think like me'. It's very hard to carry on disliking someone that clearly likes you. Like all great equations, it works just as well the other way round. If you start liking people more, maybe the'll start liking you more back.

Do not make the mistake of confusing increasing rapport, with being over-familiar. I'm not talking about being over familiar, or not giving feedback, or dropping standards to avoid discomfort or confrontation. I'm talking about being more interested and opening up to even more rapport.

Some people tell me its not necessary to know the private, personal stuff. 'We're professionals and it's non-essential'. I have a brief, they have a brief, there is a job to be done and you just get on with it.

I have a different view. I think you can only achieve so much with that model. The trouble is, when events like disappointments, unexpected change, unintended irritations or broken promises start to turn up and there is not a culture of trust and communication, often the only available route is one of greater disengagement. You can achieve 'Good' but you'll never get to 'Great'.

Favourites

I've got very clear memories of when the company I was in first introduced a new appraisal system. I was a manager at the time and to my and my fellow colleagues horror, the new idea was to allow staff to give feedback to us, the managers. At the time, this was unheard of. The Head of HR however looked very pleased with herself, but the rest of us were all bricking it.

I didn't say so to my colleagues at the time, but I actually felt I would fare quite well. I had a good rapport with my team and felt reasonably confident my feedback would be pleasingly positive.
Well, was I in for a bit of a surprise! The main feedback I got was 'David has favourites'. My jaw hit the floor and I couldn't believe it. I felt betrayed and hurt by my own team. 'How could they possibly say that'. 'That just isn't right' I insisted. 'Maybe they misunderstood the question'. After I managed to get over myself and started to look at the feedback, with slightly less defence and greater curiosity, a very useful insight and a valuable lesson emerged.

What I realized, was in any team there will be some people that I naturally get on with and those that I get on with less so. This will show up in every day innocent things like; how I say hello. I didn't even stop to think about it, but some would get a warmer hello than others. I'd enquire about weekends, families and hobbies with those that I felt more comfortable with. I'd ask for informal input or comment on ideas or plans I was considering from people I trusted a little more.

Little did I realize, I was creating my own rapport hierarchy and one of the things I hate most, an inner and outer circle. I've since learnt to be aware of that and override my desire to have most rapport with those I feel most rapport with. Everyone deserves my respect and rapport. It's my job to make sure everyone gets it. It will look different for each person, but it shouldn't feel different.

Levels of Rapport

Rapport happens on a number of different levels. It could be anything from sharing pleasantries, talking about the weather or talking about what really motivates you, self-disclosing your personal goals in life, or sharing memories of your proudest moments.

On the following page, I have provided a very simple but elegant model that distils the essence of the different levels of rapport.

LEVELS OF RAPPORT

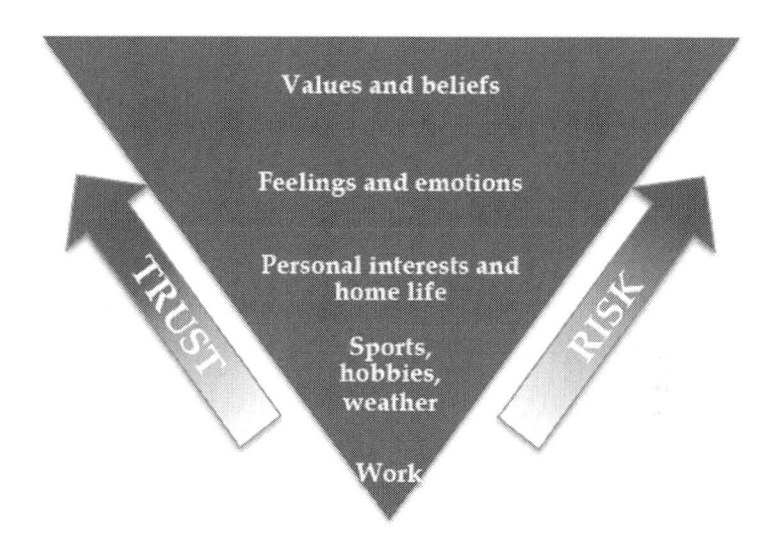

Values and beliefs

Feelings and emotions

Personal interests and home life

Sports, hobbies, weather

Work

TRUST   RISK

(Figure 13 - Levels of rapport)

The further you travel up the inverted pyramid, the greater the levels of rapport and trust you will experience and share.

'Remember, to the Limbic brain, Rapport = Trust and Acceptance. They are the two powerful gargoyles that sit either side of the gates to Engagement.
If you don't pass through these two, you're not getting in.'

The diagram is also indicating that the higher you go up the pyramid, the greater the risk also. But why would it be riskier, if you are also feeling a greater sense of trust, the higher you go up?

It boils down to what comes first. It's easy to talk about the weather or why Manchester United should never have beaten Arsenal. I don't have to self-disclose anything of myself at all, we are just talking about stuff.

Don't underestimate it though, this simple exchange of banter or pleasantries puts you firmly on the ladder and already indicates a certain level of rapport and appreciation. Some people don't even to get to enjoy that.

The further up the pyramid you go, the greater the level of self-disclosure is required. The greater the level of self-disclosure, the greater the risk and consequence of rejection, disapproval or disagreement. One doesn't come without the other. Some of you will already be very good at this, but just in case, here are a few questions you can slip in to your conversations to help create a little more rapport and elevate you further up the pyramid.

> What is your vision for yourself?
> What's really important to you?
> What achievement are you most proud of?
> What do you feel most strongly about?
> What do you feel is your greatest strength?
> What are your biggest concerns?
> What do you want to be remembered for?
> What gives you the greatest satisfaction at work?
> What does a good day at work look like?
> What do you like most about working here?
> What do you dislike most about working here?
> If you ran the place, what are the main things you would change?
> If you knew you couldn't fail, what would you do?
> How do you find working with me?
> Why do you choose to work here?

Most importantly, I use these two phrases as my guide:

> *'Leaders are called leaders because they go first'*
> *'Relationships start by giving'*

The degree to which I am willing to self-disclose first, determines how much I am going to get back. Do not use these questions as a technique. You will be found out and will end up in a poorer place than when you started. Simply build them into some of your conversations because 'You're interested, very interested'.

Are you available for rapport?

Sometimes if I am overworked, preoccupied with stuff, in a mood or just too busy being important, I simply don't have the time or the inclination for rapport. Rapport is nice, but right now I've got a job to do. I think a lot of us can fall into this trap from time to time.

Being unavailable for rapport can also be a way of punishing each other, if the other party has displeased us or done something that caused us embarrassment or irritation. Women in particular (ok, us guys too) are past masters of this dark art. For example, let's say I notice that Sylvie is acting a little funny towards me, she's not quite her usual bubbly self. In my innocence I'll ask 'Are you okay?'. 'I'm fine' she says in a slightly cold-shoulder style. 'Are you sure?' I enquire further. 'No, I'm fine', she responds haughtily. I slowly begin to realize that something is wrong and that I'm now being given the 'withdrawal of rapport' treatment. I have now learnt, as many of us have, that this is a clear sign that I get to the bottom of problem and make things right, fast, or we are going to be in for a protracted mood. I think we are all familiar with that, or a version of that. Have you ever found yourself doing that, or have found yourself on the end of the 'withdrawal of rapport treatment'?

In a work context, this can be quite common.

If a manager notices that a member of their team has either become disengaged, has annoyed them by missing a key target or has let them down in some way, this potentially becomes a negative EVENT. The manager has arrived at a decision point. She or he can either:

Engage and communicate, with a view to discussing the issue, dropping it, moving on and enjoy their rapport again
                              or
Give them a negative label and withdraw rapport for a period

This act of providing a negative label and withdrawing rapport for a period, can provoke further disengagement. One of the limbic mind's greatest fears, is expulsion from the tribe. Withdrawal of rapport runs deep and stimulates this rejection-anxiety. Trust is the primary casualty if not handled well.

I was once shown something by one of my great mentors, Robert D'aubigny. It made a huge difference to me at the time and has remained with me ever since. It's one of those simple ideas that explains and clarifies so many other everyday experiences and puts life events into perspective. I call it 'The Great Circle' and it relates directly to what we have just been talking about. The idea initially looks rather simplistic, but I promise you, it has hidden depths.

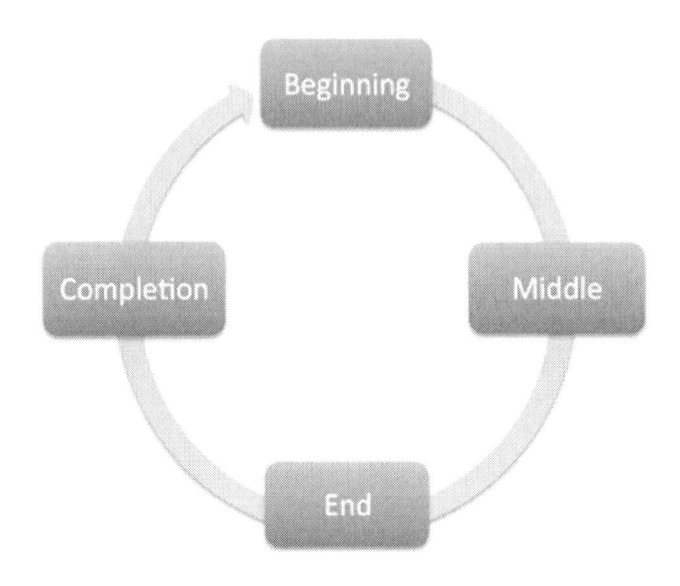

The Great Circle
The beginning

All things begin with a new beginning; relationships, jobs and even change itself, to name but a few. We love new beginnings. They are exciting, pristine and full of possibility and hope.

Have you noticed how young babies in particular, receive amazing feedback all the time. Wherever they go, all they get is kissed, cuddled, adored, cherished and told wonderful things, all the time. Even the not so pretty ones get told how beautiful they are. All is good, all is bliss. They can to nothing wrong. Throw your dummy out of the pram, three people at once leap to help retrieve it. Someone immediately pops it back into your mouth, with the most loving of words and softest of tones. Pooh yourself and everyone is interested and providing praise. Everything you do is great. Completely mess up with a show of total incompetence, by sticking a spoon up your nose and all you get is praise. 'Oh look, he's trying to eat. Well done, ooh you're going to break some hearts you are'. All of this happens because you're new! You are at the beginning of your great cycle. Personally, I don't have any memories of that. I can't remember back that far....I missed the best bit. Damn. All I know, is that it's a hell of a lot tougher now and the spoon up the nose trick doesn't draw that same gasp of admiration!!

The same is true of relationships. There's nothing like that 'new bit'. It's brilliant. Do you remember that moment when it suddenly started to dawn on you, that you are actually falling in love! It's amazing. Who's going to say it first! You are nervous, excited and feel deeply alive. Everyone loves that part of a relationship.

I even know one or two people that love that part of the relationship so much, that as soon as they start to feel that stage wearing off, they are off looking out for the next one. An endless succession of new beginnings! Probably rather tiring after a while.

Companies and organisations also love their new beginnings. They are good at them too. Every year or so, a new programme is launched, a new theme, a new transformation. We all have to learn the new language, behaviours and values. An endless procession of launches and new beginnings. By the way, I'm not knocking this at all. Change, innovation and fresh approaches are a prerequisite and essential to staying ahead of the game. The trouble happens when you launch new stuff on top of old stuff, before it is properly put to bed. It creates cynicism and tiredness.

We are all familiar with the energy, hope and aliveness that comes with new beginnings.   People go on holiday to recapture this experience, join new companies, watch films, start hobbies and enter new relationships. It's powerful juice and tastes great.

The Middle

The middle bit can be less exciting, but not necessarily so. It's the getting on with it and making it work section. This doesn't have to be boring at all, by any means of the imagination. Making this section of the cycle fun, thrilling and exciting, is an essential skill for great leadership. Things that definitely help drive that experience during this stage of the cycle are:
    Creating and maintaining a compelling purpose
    Inspired and positive managers
    Clean relationships
    Short cycles of achievement
    Genuinely empowerment to improve the business

Recognition and acknowledgement
Thanking
Activated positive values
Fun and involvement
Switching on the social dimension
Development and opportunity

The End

There comes a time when all things come to an end. In its fullest cycle, of course, 'The Great Circle' carves out the beginning, middle and end of our own lives.

Even a humble set of golf clubs, for example, goes through the same cycle. There was the 'beginning', where after much research and assessment, they are finally purchased and probably housed in an equally new golf bag. Maybe a new golf umbrella or a new pair of golf shoes will join the clubs as well. New things tend to attract other new things and like a magnet draw other new things too them. The clubs will then enter the middle of their life, once the 'I'm still getting used to my new clubs' excuse starts to wear off. The middle will last a few years, during which time there will be many moments of winning, losing, jubilation, crushing defeat, friendship and much banter. Before you know it though, a new set of shiny clubs will appear on the horizon, bring new hope of lower handicaps and better scores. The old clubs finally get replaced and for some reason usually end up in the garage or attic. The same is true of old handbags, hats or many other items for that matter.

We don't like endings and often resist them. We have a tendency to deny them or push them to the back of our minds. We put off the moment or we pretend they are not happening. Some of the things that have gone well past their usefulness or shelf-life, get stored in a garages or attics, just in case we need them again. There are cupboards and bottom drawers all over the world full of stuff that should have been thrown out years ago, but are still there. There are old suits which will never make it back to the light of day, shirts with unfashionably huge colours and shockingly bad ties. They all died a death many years ago, but we hang onto them just in case.

Some people find themselves in relationships that have ended, but they are still there, going through the motions. Some people are in jobs that they should have moved on from, but haven't. Some people are sporting hair-styles that should have been terminated many years ago. We don't like endings and if we are not careful, we let things go well beyond their sell-by date and as a consequence, diminish our energy and our zest for life.

Completion

The last part of the circle (not that a circle has any real beginning or end) is the Completion phase. Other words for completion are:

Letting go
Acknowledging
Forgiving
Bringing to a close (closure)
Creating the space for the new
Resolution
Add the final touch

Completion is an experience, as opposed to a thing. It lies in the realm of feeling. It's like a letting go, a final out breath.

Without fully completing something, it's not possible for something truly new to turn up. Many people have told me about relationships or jobs they left because of unresolved issues, only to find the same character or problem turn up again, only in a different form.

It's a bit like karma.

'If you don't complete the past, it will show up again in your future'

Apart from being very interesting and worthy of a book or two, how does this relate to Engagement and Rapport? It relates particularly to not completing things and leaving things incomplete. As I have matured, I am becoming increasingly aware and sensitive to INCOMPLETIONS.

Incompletions are those things that should have been done by now, but haven't. By this I mean all the things that are incomplete in your life, that you haven't got around to yet. Here are some simple examples: your home (light bulbs that need replacing, draught excluders that needs changing, cleaning the kitchen cupboards, removing junk from your garage and attic etc.), your finances (set up a savings account for kids, write a will, sort out tax etc), your health (full check up, visit the dentist, join a gym, get a juicer etc). This also includes your relationships: your friends and family (reconnect with your old best friend, throw a party, tell your dad you love him, take you mum out and give her a special day etc), and your work (unfinished reports, appraisals, organizing a team social event, bringing all emails up to date).

I strongly suggest you make a list of your incompletions and start to attack them one by one. You'll be amazed, as I was, how much energy it releases. Use the headings I've mentioned above and think of as many as you can.

The important thing about incompletions is that they absorb energy, they hold you back. In and of themselves, each individual incompletion doesn't suck up that much of your energy, but put them all together and they can soak up huge amounts of your life force. As my friend Woody used to say:

'Maybe you're tired, not because you're a Piscean and Neptune is entering Uranus, maybe you've just got a lot of incompletions!'

He's right. A lot of incompletions can totally drain you and strip you of your 'Pep' and 'Whizz'. If you write the lists as I suggest and just step back for a moment to look at them, you will probably notice a huge fog of apathy surround you. Even the thought of tackling that lot saps you of all your strength! That's how much of your energy is tied up and hijacked by them.

We all know of the marvellous release we experience when we finally complete something. I eventually got around to oiling some decking at my place recently. Every time I walked on or past that decking, a little bit of me knew I should oil it, especially as winter was coming. Every time I put it off, or came up with an excuse, however plausible, a little bit of my energy got zapped. I did this many times. When I finally got around to doing it, not only did I enjoy it and feel a great sense of achievement, I felt noticeably lighter and more energetic. That's what happens.

There was a phrase a friend of mine used to use, that I did not really understand. It didn't seem to make logical sense. 'If you want to get something done, give it to a busy man'. In the light of my new understanding of 'Completions', it now makes complete sense. Some people are good at recognizing when things are incomplete and they immediately act on them. They understand the value of completing things. In the same way, you can walk into someone else's house and the whole place is a total tip. There are incompletions everywhere you look, tread and smell. 'Why don't you tidy the place up?' you may ask. 'I don't have the time' they'll tell you.

Becoming more sensitive to and acting on incompletions at work, is an important part of building engagement. Any Event that happens, that is not completed in some way, becomes an incompletion.

Let's say the policy of subsidizing food at the staff restaurant is changed, due to the last round of budget cuts. Meals are now much more expensive and I have to meet the increase out of my own pocket. Imagine I don't have a particularly good rapport with my manager and they look far too busy to be bothered by my personal grievance. I may run the risk of them thinking I'm just having a moan or consider me negative. I now have a barrier to completion and closure. Since it's outside of my comfort zone, I don't want to talk about it directly, in case I get in trouble; I don't want to leave either, as it's not that big a deal. The only other option left open to me, is to allow the event to take me a little further down the disengagement route. I'll end up having a good moan to my mates about greedy managers and the cynical erosion of benefits for the people who are doing all the real work.

Bert had a great way of handling this. He was very sensitive to incompletions and would notice if anyone in his team were unhappy about something. He'd mention it and talk it through to completion. After a while, we also got used to recognizing incompletions and would get more proactive with bringing the conversation to him. Bert was easy to talk to. He was very available to rapport and created a culture where it was OK to talk.

One or two people took advantage at first and would bring everything to him, even the slightest thing. Bert was quick to point out the difference between completing things and just moaning (in a nice way). The point is: one way to complete little things is to just let them go; acknowledge it, move on and consciously let it go.

Bert also recognized that some leadership decisions would probably play some staff off-side. He would head these off at the pass by proactively forewarning his team what was about to happen and would talk it through to a point where we could all let it go, before it became a big issue.

'Events that remain incomplete or are not completed satisfactorily, induce people to go down the Path of Disengagement. An atmosphere of genuine rapport and two-way communication allows closure, resolution and a return to greater engagement'

Without Rapport, there is not the trust or the will required to tackle incompletions effectively. This is why Rapport is so critical to creating excellent engagement.

Are you available to Rapport? is a bit of a closed question. Perhaps a better question would be: could you be more available to rapport?

Whilst I like to think I'm a friendly chap, unless I make time in my diary for just hanging out with my team, spending time on the front line, telling stories, getting to know people, their lives, their families, it just doesn't happen as powerfully as it could. Do you always take the longest way round to your desk and say "Hi" to as many people as possible? Do you go around and thank everyone on a Friday for a great week, irrespective of individual wins or results?

There's nothing worse than watching a Director from Head Office dash into a regional office, rush immediately to their meeting and then dash off a couple of hours later without saying hi to anyone apart from maybe the 'important person', the site manager. That sends out a very unhelpful message, but sadly a lot of people do it.

Respect and Rapport

Ideally, what you want is a good balance between respect and rapport. Both are important.

When I was growing up, I respected my father. If I didn't, I would feel it, if you know what I mean. Fathers required respect and it was not something I or we questioned. It was very much the culture and we all went along it. Whether or not I had any rapport with my Dad was very much down to his mood at the time!

With my son Harrison, thirty or forty years later, the opposite is true. I don't particularly require him to respect me, that's something I earn, but I do expect to have a good rapport with him.

I think all of us over a certain age have experienced that huge sea-change. Probably the sixties had a lot to do with it, where the dismantlement of barriers and taboos between generations and society as a whole, were dramatically accelerated.

In the same way, we have seen a change between generations, I can see the same theme running through the relationship between managers and staff. Even the titles we give the various parties are changing to reflect that. It used to be managers and subordinates and now its team leaders and associates.

Back in the early eighties, as a young and newly promoted manager, I was advised in order to be effective and command respect, I should do the following: (read this with a 1940's British accent)

Keep a healthy distance from staff
Avoid tittle-tattle
Look slightly irritated and dissatisfied, keeps them on their toes
Carry a file or paperwork under one's arm, always appear busy
Point out areas of dissatisfaction and inadequate standards
Speak clearly and with unquestionable authority
Too much listening is a sign of weakness and should be limited to the job at hand
Operate on a need-to-know basis
'Fire one to impress a thousand'

Following this recipe of how to control lazy good-for-nothings was the order of the day and a sure-fire way to impress my seniors and make my way up the organisation. This is a rather British example, but I'm sure it translates well across all borders. I may have exaggerated slightly, but depending on where you worked, it's probably not that far off. Go back another fifty years and it gets even more draconian. Wow, how things have changed!

Since then and now, the balance between Respect and Rapport has fundamentally shifted. In the past, respect was more highly valued than rapport. I believe we have now arrived at a place where rapport is now valued above respect. In fact, the route these days to respect lies to some extent in the degree to which you are willing to extend rapport.

As a point of clarity, this does not mean that disrespect is now OK. As well as extending rapport to others, as a means of gaining respect, a good deal of respect lies in your values and the degree to which you genuinely live by them.

When I say have deeper rapport with your staff and get closer to them, it does not mean: getting so drunk on a team night you can't remember anything that happened, having serial affairs with the people you manage, gossiping or openly mocking other departments or the leadership.Improve your rapport, don't lower your standards.

I know nowhere where this change has happened more than in India. When I first worked there in 2000, the management style was firmly down the autocratic end of the spectrum and obedience was mandatory. All managers were male, had large well developed moustaches and had an aptitude for bossiness. Fear was a good motivator and rapport was not a button that existed on many manager's consoles. It was effectively off the menu.

I myself, was treated like a mini Maharaja and was deferred to, as if almost a semi-godlike being. I found it very uncomfortable and I'm sure the staff didn't like it either. However, that was the culture of the time and that's the game we all played.

What I found most interesting was that outside of the work environment (and sometimes in it, when the manager wasn't around), you would witness people who possessed an extraordinary capacity for rapport, playfulness and a lightness of being. The absence of any cynicism, mixed with the abundance of innocence, positivity and humour, was absolutely breathtaking. However, place these wonderful people in a call centre, give them a script and some good old-fashioned medieval management and you have the perfect ingredients for a disaster.

Fifteen years later, on my last visit, what a difference! I am treated like a normal human being, many managers are now female and you can feel the confidence of the whole country has risen. Interestingly, staff turnover in many operations has reduced significantly. Over that period of time, far greater emphasis is now placed on innovation, creativity and rapport. You would never have seen this back in the year 2000.

In the next chapter, we will be exploring how some of this old 'manager-subordinate' language is still very common today. Without realizing it, it can reduce our ability to create rapport and engagement and will put the brakes on the potential of your team.

'Being in service is different to being servile.
Our finest leaders know and respect that.'

As well as money, rapport is why many of us go to work, it's what we look for when we gather, it's what builds marriages, friendships and many of the best things in life. Rapport is the gateway engagement. Would you be willing to increase the level of rapport you are offering and enjoying, at home and at work? Are you willing to open your door wider and let more people in?

There are many powerful techniques that have been developed over the last thirty years that can help to build and create better rapport. The very best are encoded in the now popular science of NLP (Neuro Linguistic Programming), initially founded by the two linguistic geniuses, John Grinder and Richard Bandler and indeed many others since. I was fortunate to work with John Grinder in Santa Cruz during the summer of 1992. If you haven't already, I would urge you to explore these communication breakthroughs for yourself. They are very effective and will help to extend your ability to influence, inspire and make magic happen. I have listed some useful resources for you at the end of this book.

Motive

The most powerful Sphere of Influence is MOTIVE

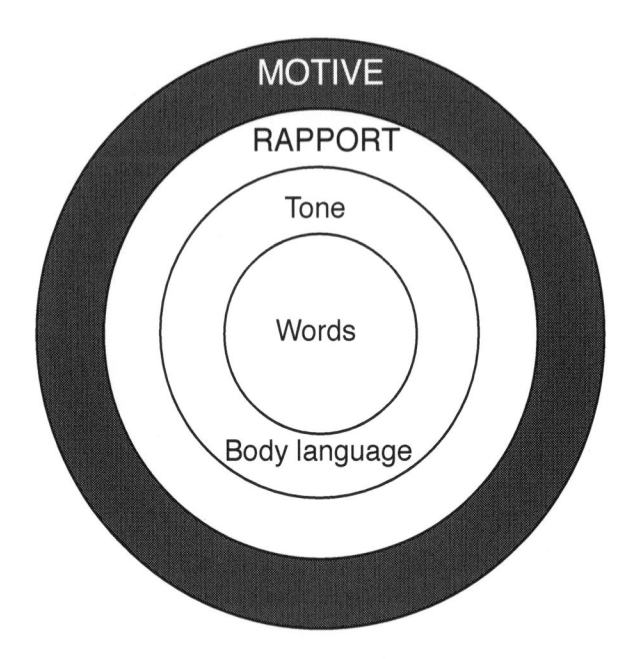

(Diagram: concentric circles labelled from outside in — MOTIVE, RAPPORT, Tone, Words, Body language)

By motive, I mean 'The motive I imagine you have towards me'.

Matters concerning motive are constantly monitored by the all seeing limbic brain. If you think back to our ancient primate roots, it was fundamental to our survival to be able to accurately survey and correctly assess the intentions and motives of fellow primates, predators or other animals. Do you want to eat me or collaborate with me? Are you friend or foe? Are you an insider or outsider? Our lives depended on this ability to judge and respond to the motives of others. Collective members of your tribe would depend and rely on your talents in this area too, especially if you were on look-out duties!

When it comes to survival, Motive is king and over trumps even the mighty Rapport. We are all very sensitive to motive, or more accurately, 'IMAGINED MOTIVE'.

The limbic brain forms its opinions on the basis of feelings, emotions, body language and first impressions. It does this very quickly and as a consequence doesn't always wait for all the facts.

Once it has formed an opinion, it then goes on a search for evidence to prove its original point correct, to support it and back it up. It 'self-convinces' itself. The Limbic brain has a strong desire to be right. It prefers black and white, right and wrong. As Prof. Steve Peters puts very eloquently in his book 'The Chimp Paradox', the Limbic brain can be paranoid and irrational. It has an overriding requirement to feel safe, therefore it is vigilant and is continually looking out for danger. It thinks that it is safer to be a bit paranoid and wary towards others, rather than relax and potentially risk its life. It worked perfectly well for our ancestors back then and proved its effectiveness many times over. There was, therefore no reason to discard it. In fact, as we saw in the first chapter, quite the opposite. Evolution saw to it that this highly successful awareness and set of behaviours was retained and occupies a central seat of governance within our modern contemporary brains.

This goes some way to explaining why rapport and motive are so powerful. Clearly, our ability as managers and leaders to engage successfully in these powerful Spheres of Influence, really is where the game is won and lost. It is a wonder that these aspects of communication are given so little attention, especially Motive, in management and leadership development.

Let me run a few examples past you, to demonstrate Motive in action and allow you to consider this insight in more detail.

Motive and feedback

Bert, or St Bert, as I feel I should now call him, was very good at maintaining a very clean and positive motive towards his team members and the other people he interfaced with. Because of how he encouraged and engaged with me, I had a very clear impression of what his motive was towards me:

'He wanted my life to turn out great, he wanted me to be the best I could possibly be, he wanted to grow and develop me and I felt pretty certain he really liked me'. That is a very positive motive.

Bert was a very honest man and as part of his style, he often liked to give regular feedback. Most of his feedback was positive and encouraging and some was related to advice or coaching, aimed at solving technical or more delicate business matters.

Occasionally however, it was direct personal feedback, addressing something he was unhappy about or something he felt I could improve on, or something I could just do with hearing. As I experienced, with a good level of certainty, that he had a very positive motive towards me; when I received his feedback I would always:
- Lean forward
- Listen intently
- Ask clarifying questions
- Maybe take a note or two of key points and actions
- Thank him at the end
- Start making changes as soon as I left his office
- Keep our discussion to myself and demonstrate my understanding through my actions

A week or two later, Bert would signal he'd seen change (or not as the case may be).

I've also had one or two bosses where I sensed they had a totally different motive towards me:

'They don't care about me, they don't even know the names of the people closest to me, my wife and my son. They wouldn't have a clue. But, they want me to get good results, to make their results look good, for their boss. I'm just a pawn in their boss-focused game. Besides which, I don't think they even like me. I'm certainly not in their special inner circle'.

If they try to give me some similar personal feedback, I'm going to treat this very differently:
- I'm not leaning forward; I'm now leaning back in my chair, sporting a 'whatever' face
- I'm mainly listening to the commentary in my head, as opposed to them: something along the lines of 'I can't wait to get out of here to tell all my mates what a complete !****! you are'
- I'm not asking questions, I'm providing excuses, disagreeing or staying outwardly silent
- I don't thank them at the end, I slink or storm out
- As soon as I leave their office, I'm looking for my mates to have a damn good moan
- I don't keep it to myself, I'm now recruiting people to agree with my version of events

A week or two later, we are still avoiding each other.

I remember one time when Bert invited me into his office and he said 'David. My PA told me this morning that she saw you playing cards on your mobile phone during office hours. As far as I know it was your lunch-break, but that's not the point. In light of how I'm trying to develop you as a Director, I feel let down that I have to mention something as trivial as this. Believe me though, it's the trivia that will let you down and it's what gets talked about. How's Harrison's drumming coming on?...' It wasn't a particularly big thing and the subject matter was more of a useful tip than a career-defining intervention. However, it was typical of the man and his excellence around maintaining a positive motive:

> I knew he had a positive motive towards me, so I was willing to listen to his feedback, get it and get on with fixing it. He told me straight away, so it reinforced my belief that he was truthful, doesn't keep things to himself or store things up for an unpleasant surprise later on. He openly identified the source of his information, showing his confidence in a culture of openness and nullifying any suspiciousness or witch-hunt I may want to mount on leaving his office. As soon as he said it and saw I'd got it, he dropped it. In other words, we completed it. We created space for something more interesting to turn up. I knew he liked and respected me, as he allowed me to instantly save face by moving the subject on to something more positive and meaningful. He knew Harrison by name and that drumming was his passion. Most importantly, he reinforced his motive towards me, right in the heart of some corrective feedback; 'I'm trying to develop you as a Director'.

Bert didn't go on a course to learn all that.

'That's what naturally comes out of your mouth when you have a positive motive towards someone'

Good parenting is not that different. It's the loving motive that allows all those lessons and all that guidance to seep in.

During the rebellious years, teenagers soon learn that Motive can act as the ultimate weapon and they use it to strike at the emotional heart of their enemies (us poor parents). 'You hate me, you're trying to stop me, you want me to be something I'm not, you never give me what I want' ...and the rest. Teenagers are not stupid. It doesn't take them too long to work out that Motive is king and gets the best results, fastest. Girls learn this quicker than us boys. Dads are utterly defenceless, resistance is futile.

Motive and service

Motive doesn't just influence relationships within organisations, it equally affects an organization's relationship with its customers as well. Customers have equally well-tuned limbic minds, which are on the look-out for motives. This is particularly heightened when it comes to the matter of service. These are often referred to as 'moments of truth'. As a customer, if you call a contact centre, can you tell the motive the agent has towards you? Are they just going through the motions? Are they just trying to sell to you? Do they genuinely want to help you?

Can you tell? Damn right you can. It's obvious. Your Limbic brain has probably made its mind up in the first 10 seconds.

Let's imagine I want to find out what the value of my pension is. I am approaching the age when pension value is important to me and I want to make sure all is in order. This is not calling up to order a take-away, this is a big deal. There is a lot riding on it. I am anxious and hopeful.

Scene One:

Agent:	'[In a flat voice] Pensions, how can I help?'
Me:	'Oh, hello, I'm David Coleman... I was hoping to find out the value of my pension fund please?'
Agent:	'I need to take you through security, what's your last name and account number?'
Me:	'Coleman. 1234567'

Scene Two:

Agent:	'[In a vibrant voice] Good morning, I'm Jo Roberts in Pensions, How can I help?'
Me:	'Hi Jo, I'm David Coleman...'
Agent:	'Hi David'
Me:	'I'm hoping to find out the value of my pension fund please'
Agent:	'Certainly, in that case, what I'd really like to do is quickly get you through your security and I'll make sure you get all the information you'll require'.
Me:	'Thanks Jo. Make it a big number...please!'

Can you tell which one is just going through the motions and which one really wants to help me? Of course you can. It's written in big red writing above their heads. As human beings, we are all super-sensitive to other people's motives, it's one of the things we are innately good at. The vast majority of us are really excellent at this.

Let's look at this through the coaching or training window.

On hearing the first 'obviously going through the motions call', the wise manager immediately recognizes that this is above all, a matter of ENGAGEMENT. They know that people only say things like that and sound like that, if they are well down the Path of Disengagement. Before going anywhere near helping them with the specifics of how their word choice and tone could be improved, they would start to explore what led to their poor state of mind.

On hearing the first 'obviously going through the motions call', the inexperienced manager would be immediately coaching on specifics 'You need to sound more positive', 'On the next call have more energy and put a smile in your voice'. 'Try this, try that'.

There is no point giving someone feedback if they are not in the mood to hear it. This is why coaching people who are well down the Path of Disengagement is so awkward and unsatisfying.

'Engage with Disengagement first and the tone will follow.
It doesn't work the other way around'

The genius of Bert - an elephant never forgets

Whether he realized it or not, Bert possessed a bunch of keys that opened the doors to engagement. The largest of the keys on his keyring was the thing that set him apart.

It wasn't so much what he did, it was more of a case of what he didn't.

If, or when someone in his team didn't respond positively to an Event and allowed themselves to go down the Path of Disengagement, even if they went way, way down there, he wouldn't do what most would. He wouldn't get sucked in and start to view them as what they had now become.

> *'Bert remembers everyone is an 'A',*
> *no matter how they may look or behave.*
> *They always were, they always will be.*
> *He was not deceived by outer appearances'*

He would talk to them 'as if' they were an A, treat them like they were an A and keep that going until the person remembered their own true nature. That's not so easy when you have someone in front of you displaying all the outward signs of apathy, cynicism or 'whatever-ness!' The 'label production department' in the limbic brain will be doing overtime and it takes a big heart to remember a person's true nature, in the heat of a situation. It's easier as a parent (sometimes), as they are your own blood and you know them intimately. It's much, much harder when it's someone not performing and you don't necessarily have a great rapport with them. How you view a situation is a creative act. You are not just a passive observer. This is harder to remember this these days, as we are so used to switching into passive receive mode with our TVs and smart phones

> *The view we choose to adopt about any person or situation changes and determines the outcome*

People live up to the labels we give them. It's the easiest thing in the world to give someone negative labels, if they are displaying negativity. Bert was brilliant at seeing the highest in people and making that their label. He shone a light on people that was brighter than the light they shone on themselves. His genius was that he maintained a positive motive towards people, no matter what. The engagement he created was spectacular. I will never forget it.

I learnt many things from Bert, however, in hindsight, there were three things that made the most difference to me. Two were insights and one was a question.
1. I can choose to see someone as their outward behaviour, or I can choose to see them as their inner best
2. Over time, how I choose to see someone, affects what what they become

And the question, like any good question is a simple one. I found it to be very powerful and goes right to the heart of what creates engagement.

3. **Am I willing to consider upgrading my motive towards people?**

This question has transformed my own ability to get engaged and the level of engagement I enjoy with other people. Clearly, it is not a question you only ask once. This is a horse we will all fall off many times. Being willing to make this question a habit, is what will make it really work.

A good place to start when considering a question like this is to have a look at where we are now. What is your current position? What is your current motive towards the people you work with?

Write down the names of the people in your team and next to each name, see if you can tease out what you feel your current motive may be towards each of them. You may wish to list out why that is, or what may have happened for you to have arrived at this motive, good or not so. Finally, start to form what motive you'd ideally like to have towards them. Don't underestimate this. This is powerful medicine! Don't forget your boss. Motives flow up as well as down.

Why not try this out closer to home and have a look at your motive towards your nearest and dearest. Could you do a motive upgrade there as well?

Compartmentalization

I am often asked 'Is it possible to feel engaged in one area of your life and not in another?' I think the answer is certainly yes and from what I can see, it is not that uncommon. Some people seem to be very skilled at compartmentalizing their lives and somehow manage to keep one part of their life separate from another. They can go long periods of time with one area seemingly not affecting or touching the other. Sometimes you just can't afford for the not-so-good part of your life to affect the other part of your life.

The problem of course is that there is only one me. I am a whole human being and despite my best efforts, the process of osmosis takes place in the background. I won't notice it at first, but after a while, bad bits seep into good bits and it will start to show up somewhere. Maybe in my energy levels, my outlook, my sense of humour or possibly my health. I admire people that can keep things going, when a part of their life takes a dip. Ideally, I should resolve any areas where my engagement or happiness are being compromised, despite my desire to put my head in the sand.

Many people find compartmentalization very difficult and whatever happens in one part of their life affects all other parts. This works both ways, positive and negative. They fall in love and everything is great. She finishes it a couple of weeks later and the whole universe implodes! Having said that, it's far better to have one part of your life really working than let a poor part of it ruin everything. Sometimes, having a part of your life really working for you, gives you the very strength and optimism you need to tackle the difficult bits.

At work, or anywhere where you get together with people, this dynamic has a powerful effect. As we all know, one person with a bad mood or someone who persistently has a 'downer' on everything, can swing the atmosphere to the negative for everyone. As a manager or indeed as a colleague or friend, how you deal with this is will significantly alter the outcome. It will probably change how you are viewed as well.

Bert used to handle this well. Let's say a member of the team arrives at the office looking down and their first few sentences are moans and groans, all spiced with a bit of cynicism and a pinch of sarcasm. I'm sure you get the picture. Bert notices this and is naturally concerned, as they are clearly unhappy and this is going to affect everyone. He invites them for a chat to make sure they are OK. He discovers that things at home are tricky at the moment and it's been like this for some time. Bert now has a number of options and routes he could go down:

1. He could notice it, give them a 'difficult person' label and choose to avoid them but talk about them behind their back later on
2. He could notice it, give them a 'difficult person' label and pretend to show concern. He could offer them time off or perhaps an easier task, in the hope that they cheer up
3. He could notice it, suspend the desire to apply any new labels and get into rapport. Most importantly, rather than offer sympathy, lighter workloads and time-out, he would say something more along the lines of. 'Well if it's not working too well in that part of your life, let's at least make sure it's working for you here'. Bert knew that if someone can get some positivity going and get stuck in and engaged in one part of their lives, that will also rub off on the other parts. It works both ways.

That person would instinctively know what Bert's motive was in each of the possible scenarios and whether or not his rapport was genuine. Is Bert a hard man? Certainly not, he was actually very kind in nature. He's made of flesh and blood like the rest of us.

What he won't do though is buy my sorry story and accept a smaller version of me. We could all do with people like that in our lives.

As a best friend to someone, I'm sure we all go down the number 4 route, sooner or later. It may take some listening, some sympathy and possibly a few beers or glasses of wine, but at the end of the day we know the only way out, is up. You truly support someone by helping them get stronger, not weaker. That's truly respecting someone and in turn, that's what creates respect.

My mum called it 'Tough Love'. The roots of tough love lie in a positive motive and a good heart.

Naturally, if you discover that the person you are concerned about really is struggling in a serious way, you may need to involve other people that are better placed to help.

The Heart of Engagement

Motive and Rapport

A powerful motive binds people together, it unites and creates common purpose. It also has an unmistakeable ability to create deep rapport. I'm sure from time to time you have found yourself in teams or projects where there is a strong sense of purpose. Have you also noticed that with that sense of purpose, there also comes a strong sense of rapport? I have worked in teams where I have experienced a deep rapport with some people that I would never normally have been drawn to, in a more social setting. Motive has that ability. It over-trumps and to an extent, determines the level of rapport that exists between people.

My grandfather used to tell me and my two younger brothers a rather odd story, when I was a kid. I didn't really understand it back then, but I liked it. It was a story he told about the second world war and what it was like back in those days. He had failed his medical and didn't get sent to the front. Instead, he ran a bank in London and looked after the people at home. He would sit back in his armchair, draw on his pipe and fix his eyes somewhere in the middle distance, as he remembered and recounted his tale. My mum used to say it was a silly story and he shouldn't be telling it to the children. The story has stayed with me though, as it evokes something rather special and something that seems to be present in all the stories you hear about survival and hanging on together for dear life.

'You may find this strange boys, but I had some of the best times of my life in the second world war' (I think that was the bit my mum didn't like). *'You see, back then we all wanted the same thing you see, all of us. It didn't matter what job you had, or what you did, or who you knew. We all wanted to defend our country, stop the enemy and stand for what was right. You could look at anyone in the eye and you just knew it. We all wanted the same thing. Manners, you've never seen anything like it. People's manners towards each other were impeccable. You would always help where you could, nothing was too much bother. It didn't matter whether you knew them or not, didn't matter at all. We were all in the same boat. Everyone said hello to each other and if someone said how are you, you'd tell them, you'd really tell them. Everyone had the time of day*

for everyone else. Those were special times. Manners, kindness and helpfulness wherever you turned. You don't get that these days, people have no idea how good people can be. Don't get me wrong, I wouldn't wish a war for you boys. No, no, not at all. Terrible things happened, terrible. I'll never forget it.'

At this point Grandpa would usually be told to stop being silly and would be diverted back to the card game he was so fond of.

This is a story of motive and the deep rapport it creates between all people, even between strangers as Grandpa would say. Bert didn't create rapport with us by being chummy, taking us out for beers and being one of the lads. He actually did very little of that. What he did do though, was create very strong rapport and a sense of camaraderie by creating a strong motive and a clear vision for where we were all headed. A strong motive is a powerful thing. I'm sure many of you have seen that rather interesting quote from Margaret Mead, the famous American cultural anthropologist:

'Never doubt that a small group of thoughtful, committed citizens can change the world; indeed, it's the only thing that ever has'

When Motive goes bad
The Player

There is little that causes more outrage and disgust than someone, who enjoys a position of trust, is subsequently discovered to be pursuing a self-serving motive. In the same way, a manager pursuing a self-serving motive is a primary destroyer of Engagement. This gets increasingly problematic the more senior the individual becomes.

There is nothing worse, or more divisive, than a senior executive who spends more time preparing for the next meeting with their boss, than they do with their own team. They are more concerned about their own upward movement through the organisation, than they are for the very people in service to them. Indeed, many of these people may be pressed into producing many time-consuming reports and presentations, simply to further the pursuit of their own wonderful career. I name this person 'The Player'. Actually, I didn't come up with this name myself, I was told about it by a good friend of mine that was pretty expert at spotting these characters. She was an HR Director and thankfully could do something about it.

I've witnessed it a few times and have seen the widespread trouble and disengagement it causes. I would urge any CEO or Executive Team to tackle this behaviour wherever and whenever they come across it. To benefit from the higher levels of performance associated with good engagement, you will want to root this out immediately. I find a useful phrase to remember is:

> 'The skills required to get to the top are not necessarily the ones you need when you get there'

In addition to the disengagement it causes within the teams and areas overseen by this individual, this motive and accompanying behaviours will also play out in the boardroom. It will affect the rapport, trust and co-operation between other senior executives. They may start to become more wary. They will probably start to question whether they should be diverting more time to prepping for their next meeting with their boss. Co-operation turns to caginess and above all, the vital glue necessary for any successful team; 'one team, one purpose', will begin to evaporate, as limbic minds become more uncomfortable. This ego-centric, self-serving activity does not go hidden or unnoticed. Like any ulterior motive, it's hard to disguise. We all see it, we are all sensitive to it. If the senior team don't tackle it, they will be tarred with the same brush and seen as complicit in it. Engage with it. I think it's quite natural to want to progress and get on. Make sure you bring everyone else with you.

The Schmooze

Do you know anyone that doesn't talk to you for ages, but then pops up out of nowhere and all of a sudden, they are your bestest, bestest friend? It usually doesn't take too long before you realize 'hang on a minute, they don't want me, they just want something from me'. They only love me whilst I'm useful. As soon as they get what they want, off they go until the next time they want something. It's really quite off-putting. I'm sure I would have given them what they wanted if they just asked me straight. This super-show of interest and attention really isn't needed or wanted. Do it a couple times and I'll give you the benefit of the doubt. Do it more than that and I'll start to doubt your motive. Faked rapport can't disguise a self-serving motive.

The slick

The old days of hard selling has pretty much had its day. Back in the 80's, the job of the sales person was to shift as much product as possible, by any means possible. Customers were called 'punters' and the job of the salesman was to smooth-talk as many people as possible into buying their product, irrespective of whether they really needed it or not. As soon as the pen signed on the dotted line, the sales person would triumphantly howl 'Got it!!' to their colleagues and then disappear as fast as possible, in case the punter changed their mind. Some brilliant films were made of the salesmen of that time, depicting their scams, their antics and their tricks of the trade. 'Tin Men' and 'Glen Garry Glen Ross' come to mind. If you've not seen them, put them on your list.

I'm sure we can all imagine the typical sales person of that era: white socks, slicked-back hair, car keys on their desk, gum in mouth and all talk. This is a classic scenario of motives at play. The salesman is only interested in selling their stuff and their commission. It's all smiles, attention, chocolate and flowers in the beginning. The second the sale is agreed, their job is over and it's on to the next one. No more flowers and no hope of contacting them if things go wrong. This type of selling got sales a very bad name and quite rightly so.

In reality, selling is a spectrum of motives. At one end you've got 'Trying to trick people into buying things they don't want or need'. At the other end you've got 'finding out what someone really wants or needs and then making it as easy as possible for them to get it'.

The motive of sales and service people is a direct reflection of their management's motive. The best salespeople genuinely want to help. Customers have a choice and know the difference. The old approach will never get the results of a positively motivated person.

The system

I have a friend who worked out that knowing people's birthdays is a good way of gaining rapport. They set about entering all their colleagues dates into their diary and had their system prompt them when ever any of the dates came up. They subsequently extended and developed their 'rapport machine' by adding in other details such as partners, spouses and children names, as well as some of their birthdays, if they could get their hands on the data. It didn't take long before most of us realized what was going on. Their unfaltering ability to know so many dates, that even we'd forgotten, laid their plan bare. You can't fake rapport. The limbic mind is so good at detecting anything other than authentic motive and sincere rapport, that you may as well chose to genuinely like people. I'm not saying don't have a list as a prompt, that's very handy. What I am saying is when you say happy birthday, mean it.

The two-face

I was working with a company a few years ago, looking after their sales and service divisions. As with most companies, new themes or programmes came and went. At that time, engagement was the new theme on the block. All managers were being exhorted to be vigilant about their employee engagement scores. This theme was taken very seriously, so seriously in fact, that the employee engagement score featured as a sizable measure within the directors bonus award scheme. As the close date of the employee survey rapidly approached, suddenly emails were flying around chasing staff up to complete their 'voluntary' engagement questionnaires. Out of the blue, directors who had never stepped foot on the shop floor before, were now taking swathes of staff off the floor, telling them how brilliant the company was and how much everyone was being looked after. Before the first shift of the closing day for the surveys, strategy meetings were being held with front line managers to work out the final tactics for getting staff to complete surveys. You could see the mixed feelings on the faces of the poor managers. On the one hand they wanted to be loyal to their director and make their numbers look good, but on the other, they were thinking 'It's not about the numbers, it's about something completely different, something that's the opposite of what were are being asked to do'. The cynicism that created was visceral.

When it comes to engagement, you can't force it, demand it, order it, or trick people into it. You can only inspire it by being it.

Choosing to have a positive motive

It's like what Grandma used to say: *'Don't give to get, give to give'.*

In a world where engagement is becoming more and more of a material differentiator, the leaders that truly value their people are starting to emerge as the winners. We can see that from the stark figures gleaned from the studies on engagement in the chapter 'Why get engaged?'

Here's an insightful quote from Sir Richard Branson;

'Clients do not come first. Employees come first. If you take care of your employees, they will take care of the clients.' In fact, he went further than that and said 'Put your staff first, customers second, and shareholders third.'

I think it's a great quotation and one that reminds us that employee satisfaction is the primary and causative factor in customer and shareholder satisfaction. Many businesses afford disproportionate amounts of time and concern to customer and shareholder satisfaction, often to the detriment of their staff. Happy customers and shareholders are the result of staff innovation, efficiency, service and care. Forward-looking businesses are adjusting their focus accordingly.

Selflessness

A 'selfless approach' and a more collaborative vision is emerging as a better way forward for producing results and healthier profits. Progressive organisations recognize customers and staff respond far more powerfully to organisations with good intentions and genuine motives. This is increasingly true for the millennial generation (born 1982 onwards) who value collaboration, community and selflessness with a passion. By 2020, this group will make up more than half of all staff and customers.

People like to be around people they trust. Our limbic minds are constantly assessing the people and circumstances that surround us. If we perceive a person or a company to be selfish, we subconsciously back away. We are seeing this more and more. Look at how many companies are trying to sell their corporate social responsibility agendas, hoping in some way to profit on the back of it by appearing nice. Some are authentic, others pursue this quite cynically, in my view. A good example is a tobacco company's corporate social responsibility, trying to pass off as being genuinely caring. I think it's true to say that it is widely viewed as a thinly-disguised, self-serving marketing tool, primarily aimed at ensnaring new generations of users.

On the positive side, people want to associate with people and brands that are characterised by an element of selflessness. They value that deeply positive human quality and the trust it builds.

Acts of selflessness inspire deep emotions. It's as if selflessness is our true state, were it not masked by our fears. That's why we respond so strongly when we see it.

The Hollywood film industry was built on these powerful emotions. The recurrent theme of the hero, who selflessly risks their own life, on behalf of a quest or something greater than themselves, lies embedded in almost every great movie. For 'Woody' in 'Toy Story', it was for 'Andy'. For 'Superman', it was the citizens of planet earth. For Emmeline Pankhurst in 'Suffragette', it was for the rights of women. Every baddie on the other hand, is in it for their own self-glorification. They are in it for themselves.

It's much easier to work for someone that has a purpose or motive greater than themselves

In Star Trek, with their spaceship *Enterprise* in imminent danger of destruction, Spock enters a highly radioactive chamber, in order to fix the ship's warp drive engine, so the crew can escape certain death. Spock quickly perishes due to intense radiation and with his final breath, says to Kirk, '*Don't grieve, Admiral. It is logical. The needs of the many outweigh . . .*' Kirk finishes the sentence for him, '*The needs of the few.*' Spock replies, '*Or the one*'.

I could work for a Vulcan like that!

I'd like to end this chapter with a story that a very good friend of mine used to tell. His name is Mark and he is from the town of Dudley, deep in the Black Country (Midlands UK). People from the Black Country are known for a few things. Probably top of the list is their unique accent and dialect. It has resisted many of the changes from the old Middle English and has retained some ancient english words like 'thee, thy and thou'. As a close second, many people from the Black Country grew up on a tradition of endless storytelling, in pubs, homes and other gathering places. Mark was no exception and boy oh boy, could he tell a story. One of his favourites, was the story of 'Heaven and Hell'. It captures the essence of what we have been considering.

Heaven and Hell

'There was a man named George who died, and when he arrived at the 'Pearly Gates', St. Peter told him he was going to take him on a tour of heaven and of hell.

First, they took a tour of heaven. Peter and George arrived just in time for dinner. It was in a huge banquet hall and the tables were sagging with the weight of the sumptuous food. Everyone was laughing and talking and having a wonderful time. They all looked well-fed and happy. George noticed that everyone had the longest forks he had ever seen, about four feet long!

Then Peter and George took off for hell. It was still dinner time when they arrived. The banquet hall in hell looked just like the banquet hall in heaven. The tables were loaded with food. But there was no conversation taking place. Everyone looked angry and resentful. They also looked like they were starving, in spite of all of that food right in front of them. Again George noticed that, just like in heaven, everyone in hell was holding a four-foot-long fork.

George said to St. Peter, 'What's going on? It looks like the food they serve in hell is just like the food they serve in heaven, but the people in hell seem to be starving to death. They are all miserable.

'What's the difference between heaven and hell?', George enquired.

St. Peter replied, 'In hell, there's no spirit of giving or of service. In hell everyone looks out only for themselves. The people in the banquet hall in hell can only think about themselves. Their forks are four feet long, so when they pick up their food with those forks, they can't get it in their mouths. So they are starving.'

'In heaven, everyone has the same four-foot-long forks, which are far too long to feed themselves, but in heaven all they want to do is serve each other. When someone is hungry, all they have to do is ask the person on the other side of the table to use his or her fork to pick up some food and feed them. Sometimes people don't even have to ask. In heaven they feed each other. In hell, everyone is so engrossed with looking out for themselves that no one seems to think of serving someone else.

A great story.

The Language of Engagement

Our language, and in particular our word choice, reflect our inner reality, our inner experience of the moment. This holds true, when we are either speaking to other people or indeed speaking to ourselves. Language and word choice has the power to inspire, ignite, enthuse or conversely suppress, dampen or even bore to death. As a leader or manager of people, your ability in this area is paramount

They say people join organisations and leave managers. Actually, it's more than just a saying, it's straightforward mathematics. Based on studies of corporate exit interviews, this is statistically the most frequent category of answer provided as to why people leave organisations.

The top six reasons people leave organisations within this category are often given as (depending on which report you read):

Relationship with boss
Relationship with Co-workers
Bored or unchallenged
Lack of opportunity for advancement
Lack of recognition
Meaningfulness of the job

I can't help feel though that these are symptoms rather than causes. I strongly suspect what lies behind these 'reasons for leaving' are the more powerful forces of engagement or the lack of it. As I have alluded to before, I've had some bosses that have been inspiring, interesting and empowering and others that have been quite the opposite. I've done some pretty menial, meaningless jobs in my life, I'm sure we all have. Sometimes though, those jobs have been some of the most exciting, fun, growth opportunities I've ever experienced. In fact, I'd go further than that and say that they were some of the best periods of my life. I've also done some equally menial, meaningless roles and I have been bored to the point of virtual catatonia. It feels like every day I go to work, a little bit of me dies.

'It is not about how interesting the job is. It's about the context the job takes place within. When the context is poor, issues of money, advancement and relationship become a problem.'

I'm sure we've all had experiences of this. I've often seen people with very well paid, relatively interesting jobs spend the majority of their time moaning, wanting to be somewhere else and dreaming of Fridays. The trouble is, once you get in the habit of moaning and being bored, you might accidentally carry that over into your weekend! Beware. Anything practiced for long enough becomes a habit. Good for learning the piano, but not always good for happiness.

From boredom to passion

In 1982, when I was 22, I used to work in the City of London. My job was nothing to do with high finance or anything cool like that. I worked in the head office of a company that made 45 Gallon steel drums. It was a totally hum-drum job. Pun intended. I worked in a small, newly glass-partitioned office for two. Strangely, my boss's name was also Bert. He was 40 years my senior, smoked a pipe and loved Beethoven. We used to sit opposite each other, getting on with our various tasks. My job was to receive orders for steel drums from our regular customers; big oil companies, food and chemical companies, paint companies, to name but a few. Once I had received the order, I would log it in my order book and phone up the factory to place the order. That was it. That was the job. To say that I was bored was an understatement. I hated it. I'm sure if our little office wasn't so smokey, you could definitely see my soul evaporating away on a daily basis. Back in those days, in the early eighties, if you were a bloke, it was absolutely mandatory that you visit your local pub during your lunch-break and have at least two beers, sometimes more. If you didn't engage in this manly pursuit, you'd be called names. That was to be avoided at all costs. By mid-afternoon, once the beer had permeated deep into my brain, the main task in hand was staying awake. I have to admit, this was quite an assignment and on several occasions proved too tall an order! How times have changed. If anyone did that today, we'd be dismissed on the spot for gross misconduct.

It was during one of those run-of-the-mill, midday outings, that my life was about to change.
I noticed in the corner of the pub there were a group of about ten people with extremely high, almost electric energy. They were hooting with laughter, slapping each other on the back and were clearly the best of friends. Their energy was infectious and extremely attractive. I couldn't keep my eyes off them. They were having just

the sort of 'time of their lives' that I really wanted. 'Why did they look so happy? What were they laughing about? What's got into them?'. To add even greater mystery, I noticed to my surprise, they were not drinking beer, they were just drinking juice!!

Eventually after much internal debate, I overcame my reticence and said the fateful words 'Hello, I'm David.' Trying to be cool, I briefly explained I happened to notice them and wondered what business they were in. In unison, they almost pounced on me, explaining that they were running their own company and were working just around the corner. It seemed to involve the telephone rather a lot, in some way. I didn't understand this because back then, the telephone was a huge brown object that you would push to the far end of your desk, hoping it wouldn't ring. Either way, they implored me to come round and see their office and see it for myself.

A week later, following their directions, I arrived at their office. I was greeted in their reception area and then led into what was called 'the phone room'. As soon as the door opened, a rush of energy, noise, singing and uncontrolled laughter flooded the room. I'd never seen anything like it. There was a huge round table in the middle of the room with people stood around it like the knights of the round table. The middle of the table had been cut out and standing in the centre was a lady who seemed to be conducting the proceedings. They sang a song at the top of their lungs (be-Bop-a-Lula by Gene Vincent and later Elvis, as it happened), then proceeded to joyously bellow from ten down to one, pick up their phones and start dialling with more intention than I'd ever seen before.

It was like a different world, it was mad, crazy, pure lunacy. I loved it and joined a couple of weeks later. Little did I know, but I had just bumped into the very beginnings of the UK's first contact centre. To be more accurate, telephone marketing business, contact centres didn't really appear on the scene in the UK until about 1985 with Direct Line insurance. I spent two years 'on the phones', as we called it, and eventually made it to Team Leader. That was one of the most exciting periods of my life. I'd never witnessed such passion to achieve target, such emotional connection to making projects work, so many great friendships at work and such a deep sense of purpose and aliveness. I didn't know of the word engagement until many years later. This place was awash with it.

The company grew very quickly and soon had to move to larger and larger offices, to accommodate the sheer volume of business that was coming our way. We even had a TV documentary made of us called 'The second oldest profession'. People were queueing up to buy our services. Soon a lot of other businesses wanted us to help them build their own telephone contact centres and we formed a training and consulting company, populated with some of our top communicators. I remember it well in 1989 when a very sensible looking chap came to our offices and got a number of us to sign an official secrets document (these days known as a non-disclosure agreement). We had never seen one of these before. He was an officer of a major bank and was launching a totally new way of doing banking. He required total secrecy. The project was called 'Project Raincloud', later known to all as First Direct, the UK's most successful direct bank. Throughout this amazing period, all of our clients would always say the same thing without fail; 'Where do you get your people from?' This always amused us, as we all knew we were from normal backgrounds. The pay was at subsistence level, the job was repetitive, it was hard work and involved long hours.

'It wasn't where we came from, it's where we thought we were going!'

In nautical terms, a ship's attitude is it's direction, its attitude is where it's headed. It's the same for people. With no real direction, a repetitive job can suddenly seem very boring. Introduce a powerful sense of direction and some inspiration and suddenly the very same job offers growth, fun and deep satisfaction.

It's a bit like a few lads just kicking a ball about in a park. It's got no sense of direction, it's just lads kicking a ball, making noise. Put a couple of jumpers on the ground as goal posts, divide them into two teams and suddenly you've got a completely different game on your hands. Things matter more, teamwork becomes important, the energy is different and scoring counts.

You can walk into some workplaces and you can instantly feel an aliveness, connection and intention to make things happen. You can walk into others, where people are doing exactly the same type of work and the atmosphere is dull, heavy and repressive. People are looking at the clock, wishing their lives away.

Inspiration

One of the things driving the level of energy, is the level of inspiration present.

I remember attending a training session on communication skills at the company I have just been talking about. The facilitator was discussing motivation and she asked what turned out to be a rather interesting question.

'Who or What is inspiring?'

I was busy trying to come up with some names of people that are typically cited as being inspiring. She proceeded by saying, 'When I say who, I don't mean who as in people or names of people, I mean who, in terms of what type of person'. We all had various guesses, only to have our facilitator shake her head at us.

She fixed her eyes on us and said 'What's inspiring, is someone who is already inspired.'

That struck me like a bolt of lightening and has stuck with me ever since. I could see exactly what she was saying. So simple, but so true. You don't have to wait to be inspired by something, you can just choose to be more inspired. I remember that moment, that's when I decided to **be more inspired**.

Years later, when I was running my own training company with my business partner, Ian 'Woody' Woodhouse, he struck on something quite brilliant and subsequently in the space of half an hour, codified what I now call the 'Language of inspiration".

As we discussed at the beginning of this chapter, our language and word choice, without necessarily realizing it, reflect our inner reality and our inner experience of the moment. Our word choice has the power to inspire, ignite, enthuse or conversely suppress, dampen or even bore to death.

Imagine if you will, an Inspire-o-meter. At the top is 'maximum inspiration' and at the bottom 'barely alive with boredom and visible amounts of 'soul evaporation'. Half way between the two is a line delineating; above the line and below the line. Above the line you have experiences like Desire, Passion and willingness. Below the line you have experiences like Boredom, Dullness and Apathy.

That language of inspiration and Engagement

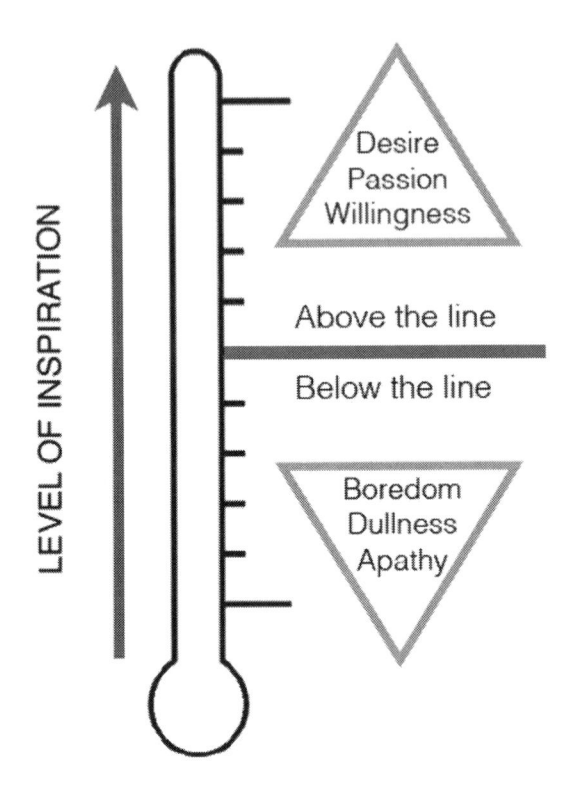

LEVEL OF INSPIRATION

Desire
Passion
Willingness

Above the line

Below the line

Boredom
Dullness
Apathy

Your inner level of inspiration and engagement is directly reflected by your language and word choice. We are doing it all the time, mostly without even realizing it. If you listen carefully to the words people use, they are constantly signalling their own level of inspiration and engagement, or not, as the case may be.

Most people, quite often as a matter of habit, tend to speak with
BELOW THE LINE LANGUAGE

It's very common. Just listen in to any conversation, TV programme or maybe a friend you're having a chat with and you will start to notice it.

The Language of Disengagement

LEVEL OF INSPIRATION

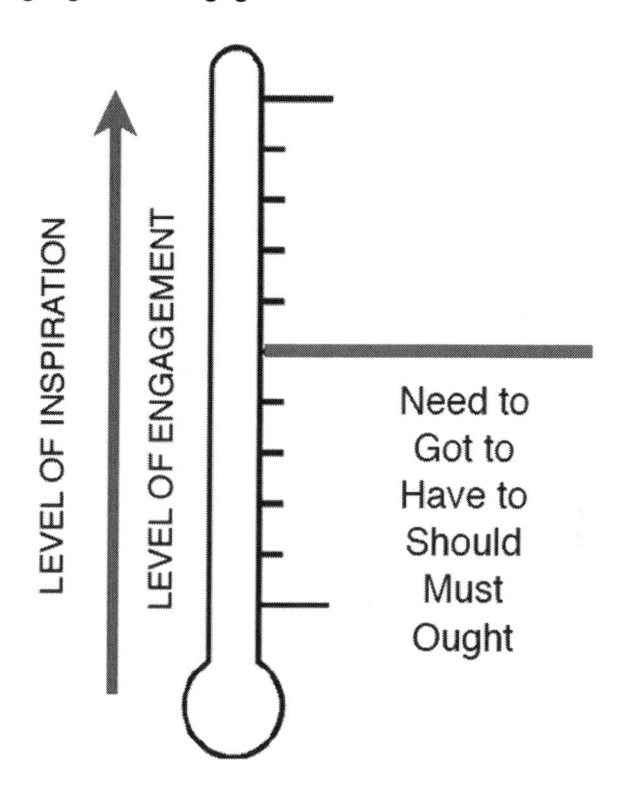

LEVEL OF ENGAGEMENT

Need to
Got to
Have to
Should
Must
Ought

These are the 'trigger words' people tend to use when they are 'below the line'. It is the language of disengagement. Nowhere is this more common than in manager-to-staff communications. Consider these phrases. Have you heard them before? Do you think you may have used them yourself?

'We **need** to improve our satisfaction scores'
'I **need** some people to help with overtime'
'We've **got** to complete the report by the end of the day'
'We've **got** to answer these calls faster'
'We **have** to reduce our errors'
'We've **got** to have more rapport with our customers'
'We **have** to sound more positive with our customers'

Endless examples of phrases containing: 'we need to, we have to, we've got to, we should, we must, we ought, we need to, we've got to, we should, we must, we ought.'

If you don't believe me, look at the last few emails you've received. Even better, look at the last few you've sent. Take a couple of moments to have a quick peek, you might be surprised!

Below the line language is the language of 'no choice': 'We pay you a salary, now you've got to do what we tell you to do'. By using the language of disengagement and no choice, you inadvertently enter the mindset of the victim. 'The world happens to me, I don't happen to it'. Below the line language is not just limited to the words I have listed above. These are the most common ones, there are many more.

Here is an example of how I can say exactly the same thing either 'Below the line' or 'Above the line'. They elicit very different responses.

'**Can't** you see what I'm saying?!' This has the effect of making the person you are speaking to automatically want to say 'No' and resist imagining what you are trying make them see. Or you could say exactly the same thing but use 'Above the line' language.

'**Can** you see what I'm saying?' You might now stand a chance of them being willing to see it. Having a positive tone, rapport and motive will also help. Get all of it positive, including word choice and you are well on the way to getting a great response.

Here is another similar example: '**Don't** you think it would be better if…?' as opposed to '**Do** you think it would be better if…?'

> *'The limbic mind has no capacity for language. It **feels** disengaged and separate when it senses below the line language and heightens its need to be more defensive and wary.'*

Your inner voice and mood

When I get up in the morning, if I'm lucky, I may get a second or two of nothing, just silence. Then the inexorable inner voice starts its chatter and doesn't stop until I go to sleep, eighteen hours later. This voice goes by many names; 'self talk', 'internal dialogue', 'the voice in my head' and many other versions of the same thing. It took me some time to recognize that I had a voice in my head. I used to think that the voice was me. I now realize, of course, that the real me has much more to do with the bit that the voice actually talks to.

How that voice talks to you is important. The tone and words it uses sets your mood, attitude and your frame of mind.

If I'm off guard, my inner voice will talk to me with below the line language. "I **have** to get up now, I **mustn't** be late, I've **got** to get the earlier train to make the meeting at the other office, I **mustn't** forget to phone Mum, I've **got** to wash my hair, the report **has got** to be completed today, I **don't** want to speak to Jerry about the shortfall, I really **should** polish my shoes etc etc. Before you know it, you are 'Below the line' and not in a great mood at all.

What I am suggesting, is that if we migrate our language 'Above the line', we can start entering the realm of 'Inspiration and Engagement.'

Going above the line

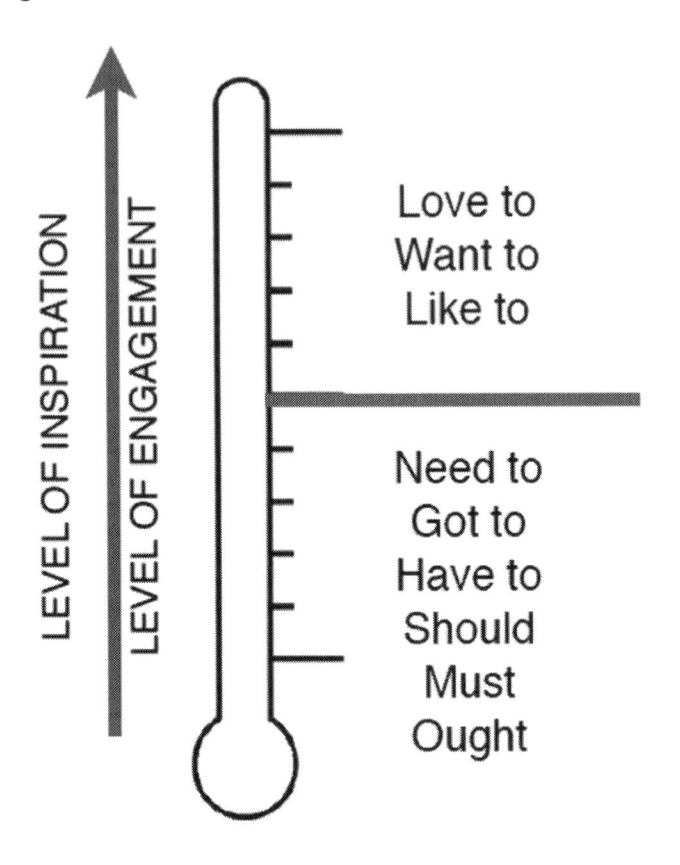

LEVEL OF INSPIRATION
LEVEL OF ENGAGEMENT

Love to
Want to
Like to

Need to
Got to
Have to
Should
Must
Ought

Above the line language naturally occurs when someone is choosing to do something, rather than feeling they have 'got' to do something. Right at the beginning of the book, in the introduction, I said 'I have always been aware that I can be two different people'. 'There's the me when I'm really firing on all 8 cylinders; I feel bright, open, naturally happy and making things happen seems effortless and fun. There's also the me that occasionally only runs on one cylinder; I can be distracted, defensive, opinionated, suspicious and sometimes the very master of procrastination and cynicism'.

In simple terms, the main difference is that I feel one way when I'm doing something because I want to do it and I feel completely different when I'm doing something because I feel I have to do it.

'This is way more than just using positive words. Above and below the line language directly signals your motive and therefore operates at the highest levels of influence.'

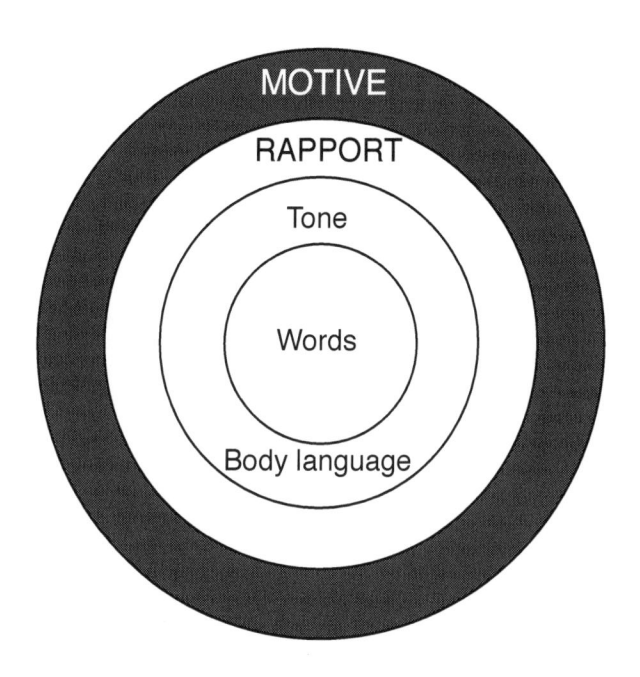

(Concentric circles diagram: MOTIVE › RAPPORT › Tone › Words › Body language)

Word choice and customer service

To understand this further, lets look at a simple interaction between a Customer and a Customer Service Agent. I'll replay the exact same example we used earlier. What you will notice is that the 'below the line' and the 'above the line' language signals completely different motives.

Scene One:
I make the call and wait in queue for about 45 seconds.

Agent: '[In a flat voice] Pensions, how can I help?'
Me: 'Oh, hello, I'm David Coleman... I was hoping to find out the value of my pension fund please?'
Agent: 'I **need** to take you through security, what's your last name and account number?'
Me: 'Coleman. 1234567'

Scene Two

I make the call and wait in queue for about 45 seconds.

Agent: '[In a vibrant voice] Good morning, I'm Jo Roberts in Pensions, How can I help?'
Me: 'Hi Jo, I'm David Coleman...'
Agent: 'Hi David'
Me: 'I'm hoping to find out the value of my pension fund please'
Agent: '**Certainly**, in that case, what I'd really **like** to do is quickly take you through your security and I'll **make sure** you get all the information you'll require.'
Me: 'Thanks Jo. Make it a big number...please!'

Can you tell which one is just going through the motions and which one really wants to help me? It's obvious, the negative or positive motive is conveyed through the Below or Above the line language.

'Whether you use Above or Below the line language affects your Tone and how much Rapport you feel like having. They act as triggers'.

An important distinction

If I say "I'd like to take you through your security", it doesn't mean you have a choice to go through it or not. Taking customers through security is not an option. All customers go through the security process. What I am saying is, not only am I going to take you through security, I'd also like to.

Consider this. If some one says 'I need to take you through security', the subtext and the meaning between the words is: I need to take you through security, because you may not be who you say you are. Prove to me that you are who you say you are. The security is for us and our protection. The Limbic Mind senses the subtext, even though it doesn't understand the superficial words. On the other hand, if someone says 'Certainly, in that case what I'd really like to do is quickly take you through your security..' The subtext, or the meaning between the words, is totally different. Not only am I going to take you through security, I'd like to as well. I want to help and I hope the fund is all you want it to be. The security is for you and I'm going to make it really quick and easy.

In a similar way, if Bert said to me 'David, I'd like you to work with Jenny to get the plan completed by Friday'. It doesn't mean that it doesn't matter if I get it in late. It does matter. He's not saying I have an option (although I could negotiate if I needed to). Not only is he asking me to complete something by a deadline, he'd also like me to as well. The subtext is: 'I'm confident in your ability, I think you can do it and I'm looking forward to it, I think it will be good'.

Bert uses 'above the line' language because **wants** to do what he is doing. He does things because he chooses to do them, not because he has to.

Being around someone with this positive approach rubs off on people. It certainly rubbed off on me, big style. It's horrible being around people who only do things because they feel they have to, especially if they are your boss! How we communicate is deeply habitual. Getting used to communicating above the line is one of the most positive practices I have ever engaged with. It's like swapping junk food for heathy fresh food. You are what you eat. You are also what you think.

Sylvie says 'Can you make me a cup of tea?'. I say, 'Darling I'd **love** to…Biscuits?' Hey, I may be heading for more than a cup of tea if I keep that up!

Experiment with going 'Above the line' for a week and just watch what happens. Prepare to be amazed! It take a bit longer than that to make it a habit, but a week of doing it will give you the encouragement to carry on. Being around a manager, or a partner, a parent or a friend or a colleague for that matter, who continually communicates below the line is a real drain. Habits are catching, don't slip below the line just because people around you have. I'm not saying never moan, sometimes a good moan sweetens a beer. My point is, ration yourself carefully. Moaning can become a way of life and has become so for many. Communication is a deeply engrained habit. Make a habit of living above the line. Train your inner voice to do the same. You'll be doing your self and the people around you a great service.

As Woody used to say, *'I want my sons to grow up in a house where they see their Mum and Dad communicating with each other and their friends 'above the line'. I think that's about the greatest gift I could give them. That's what they'll learn from most, not what I tell them to do'.*

Like changing any new habit, the first step is to become conscious of what you are already doing.

You all know the unconsciously incompetent to unconsciously competent model. This is no different. (If you haven't come across it before, look it up on the internet. It's a popular search). When you first start on your journey to use more 'above the line' language, the first thing you will notice is all those times you mess it up. That's good, that's progress. At least you are noticing it now. Don't beat yourself up if you mess up. Keep going. It doesn't matter if the odd below the line word creeps out, as long as your motive is on an upward trend, that's what makes the difference. If you are reasonably disciplined about it, it will take you about 21 to 28 days to make a positive shift. According to numerous tests and studies, psychologists agree that is the approximate time it takes to change any habit.

To create Engagement, go 'above the line'.

The Conditions for Engagement

As a keen sailor, I have developed a 'weather eye' over the years. As you would imagine, having a 'weather eye' is simply maintaining a background awareness of the current sea-state and weather conditions and remaining alert to any changes that may be developing. The reason all sailors develop this faculty is because they are acutely aware that 'the conditions' are the most important element to any successful voyage.

As I begin writing this chapter, there are a number of people preparing and training for the ARC Rally, the Atlantic Rally for Cruisers. This is an annual yachting event involving an Atlantic crossing from the Canary Islands to the West Indies. The Rally attracts about 200 boats and 1500 people each year. It usually takes about two weeks to complete and for quite a few, this will be their first ever ocean crossing.

Amongst all the varied and differing things they will be thinking about, to a person, all of them will be concerned about one particular thing - The Conditions. You can have the biggest, fastest yacht in the flotilla, the best safety equipment available and all the latest satellite communications. However, if the conditions are set against you, you are going to have a very, very uncomfortable time, possibly hazardous. A number of yachts have been lost at sea or had to be abandoned during previous rallies. Thankfully, this is quite rare, but it has to be considered when electing to participate. There was even the famous 'Cat-over-board' incident where the vessel's cat 'Choy-Choy' was asleep onboard, curled up in the mainsail. Unaware of the snoozing mouser, the sail was duly hoisted and the cat went over the side. On hearing the screech, the crew immediately executed a "C-O-B" (Cat-over-board) drill and managed to recover their pet!

In the same way, you could be making your voyage on one of the smallest boats. If the trade winds are steady, the sea is calm and the skies are clear, you will make landfall with ease, your journey will be a delight and something you will talk about fondly for the rest of your years.

Engagement is not so different. I've seen highly skilled managers struggle to create engagement because one or all of the conditions were set against them. Preparing the conditions and ensuring you are swimming with the stream is critical to a successful outcome, as opposed to continually fighting the flow of a strong adverse current.

I was once invited to take on a senior role in an organisation as their new Sales and Service Director. It was a well known international business. For me, this was a big step up and it was just the opportunity I was looking for. I felt all of my background, training and know-how were just right for the role and I couldn't wait to get started. I was excited, keen and very much up for it. As it turned out, it was a disaster. During my first week, I discovered three things:

Firstly, as part of a new company-wide programme, instigated by the Group CEO, all sales and service staff had just had all of their targets removed, not just sales targets, all targets; productivity, service levels, everything. I however, was still responsible for achieving all of them. Unsurprisingly, mayhem ensued and the operation took a significant dive across all fronts.

Secondly, prior to my arrival, a long-serving and very capable manager who had grown up man and boy with the company, had been promised point-blank by his bosses, that he would be getting the Sales and Service Directorship, as soon as the role became available. He discovered, to his absolute disgust, that the role he'd spent his entire career working towards, would not be his. This distressing realization happened the day before I turned up at his centre to introduce myself. To add insult to injury, I was now to be his direct line manager. Being an unusually strong-willed and understandably upset man, to put it mildly, he then seemed to make it his life's purpose to trip me up wherever possible and bring about my downfall.

Thirdly: having seen the clearly unworkable situation develop right before my eyes, I immediately communicated my concerns up-line and requested that the gentleman in question be allowed an honourable move to another part of the business. It was made abundantly clear to me that no other roles were available and I should work with the situation.

Three major negative events and a significant member of my team whole-heartedly committed to disengagement and proactive opposition. At that point, I should have listened to my instinct and walked away without hesitation. This just wasn't going to work. Stupidly my ego got the better of me and I decided to swim upstream. I thought with all my wonderful communication skills, engagement know-how, rapport and intention, I'd be able to win the heart of the wounded soldier and transform the bleak landscape. Nope, didn't happen.

What followed, was a year of struggle, arguments, frustration, taking sides and all sorts of nonsense. Sylvie could see a change in me too. She'd never seen me like this before.

I left after a year, well beyond my sell-by date. We did manage to achieve all of our targets by the end of the period, but to be honest, I took no satisfaction in it. I am happy to report that this individual and I have since made up and even send each other Christmas cards. The ride for him must have been as bad as mine. He was a good guy and shouldn't have been put in that position.

The following year, I was invited to take up a similar role with a similar sized organisation in Scotland, where I now live. Things couldn't have been more different. The conditions were far more favourable and we achieved more in one year than I thought we possibly could in two. We literally created magic. On top of that, I loved it and Sylvie had her happy hubby back.

Could I have played my role differently at the difficult company? In hindsight, possibly. I should have been far more insistent about the membership of my team and ensured that targets were removed gradually as we experimented with new ways of doing things. That's not so easy when you've just arrived at a new company, you are finding your feet and you don't get the support you need from above. The underlying conditions were always going to create trouble. In hindsight, I should have moved swiftly on and applied myself to something more elevating and rewarding. As they say, if it doesn't kill you, it makes you stronger!

Conditions matter. They are the context within which you operate and will exert a considerable influence on your ability to create engagement and make things go your way. Get them right and you've set yourself up, and those around you, for a win. Pay no attention to them and you run the risk of running aground.

The right conditions

Setting yourself and others up to win will happen far more easily, if you can put the right conditions in place. Let's have a close look at what they are and how to successfully embed them.

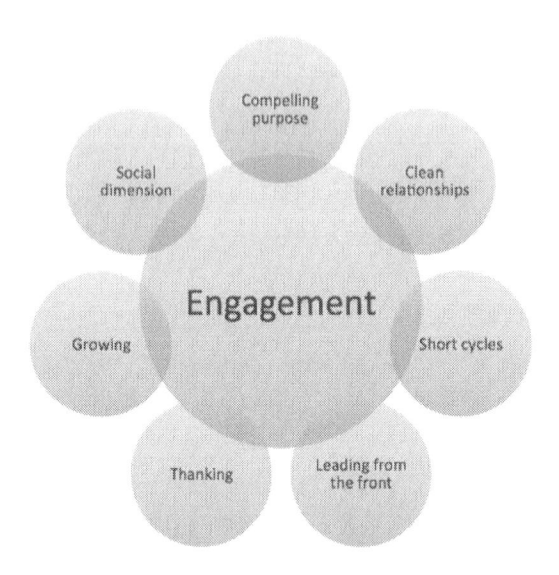

Engagement (central): Compelling purpose, Social dimension, Clean relationships, Growing, Short cycles, Thanking, Leading from the front

Compelling purpose

A lot of effort and money goes into creating vision statements and mission statements. Most organisations have them. Often the two get confused and rolled up into one thing. I have even heard them referred to as 'the poem that sits above reception in Head Office' or 'that thing on page one of the annual report'. Some are good, some not so.

Let's have a quick look at the difference.

A Vision Statement:
- Defines the ideal of what an organisation wants to achieve over time
- Provides guidance as to what an organisation wants to achieve
- Functions as the 'pole star' - it provides understanding of what everyone is working towards
- Is written in a manner that makes it easy for all employees to repeat it

A Mission statement:
- Defines the purpose of an organisation
- Answers three questions about why an organisation exists
  WHAT it does;
  WHO it does it for; and
  HOW it does it.
- Is something that all employees should be able to repeat.

These definitions are OK, but for me, they miss a vital element.

'The most important thing for any mission, vision or purpose, is that people feel it '

Fail that and they simply remain as expensive poems adorning boardrooms, receptions and annual reports. For them to contain genuine power, evoke inspiration, or drive outstanding behaviour, they should reach deep into the realm of emotion and stimulate the Limbic mind.

There is no co-incidence the two words EMOTION and MOTION are so closely linked, Feelings drive Action. Feelings drive decisions.

When I talk about this subject in workshops or facilitation events, I write the word EMOTION on a flip chart then cover up and reveal the 'E' at the beginning a few times. Give it a go on the word below. You'll see what I mean. Just stick your finger over the 'E' and reveal it a couple of times.

EMOTION

As a leader, what you want is motion. What causes that is E-motion.

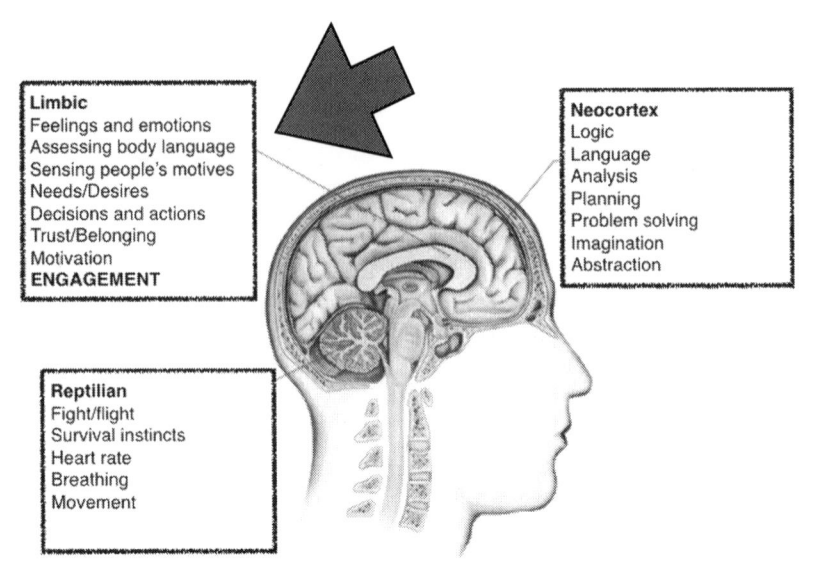

Limbic
Feelings and emotions
Assessing body language
Sensing people's motives
Needs/Desires
Decisions and actions
Trust/Belonging
Motivation
ENGAGEMENT

Neocortex
Logic
Language
Analysis
Planning
Problem solving
Imagination
Abstraction

Reptilian
Fight/flight
Survival instincts
Heart rate
Breathing
Movement

Emotion drives Motion. 95% of our actions are driven by our emotions... and that's just the logical ones of us. Anything truly motivational or something that moves us, bubbles up from the deep well-springs of our emotional centres. This then begs a few interesting questions. How do I make a vision or mission compelling? How do I endow something with emotional appeal? How do I empower an idea emotionally? How do I make something matter? How do I bring a purpose to life?

Many have answered this question. Our history as a human race is littered with exceptional people that have somehow managed to capture the hearts and minds of the rest of us mere mortals. They speak to us or relate to us at a level that literally moves or inspires us. They are not limited to a particular race, gender or creed, in fact they appear to pop up in all walks of life; business, politics, science, religion, spirituality, the helping professions, the armed forces, the arts and sports.

Sometimes they are closer to home in the form of a parent, a neighbour or a teacher. Some are even fantasy figures in the form of 'super heroes' or certain film characters. What all of them seem to have in common is the capacity to move us, or cause something deep within us to stir or even awaken. They seem to possess certain qualities that stand them apart; for some it's unusually high levels of courage, clarity or decisiveness. For others, it's great love, sacrifice, insight, compassion or just an unbelievable persistence.

When I was growing up, my heroes were Nelson Mandela, The Dalai Lama, Mohammed Ali, Carlos Santana, David Bowie (RIP), Mikhail Gorbachev, David Attenborough, Martin Luther King, Galileo Galilei,

William Wallace and of course Luke Skywalker and Spock from Star Trek, to name but a few. I'm sure you have your own list.

Now I'm thinking about it, other heroes of mine come to mind; John Pilger, the writer and broadcaster, famous for his staggering honesty and forthrightness. Hans Blix, the UN weapons inspector who stood up against so much pressure to find non existent WMDs. Germaine Greer, the feminist that just 'said how it was', Jamie Oliver, who was willing to risk his reputation and do battle with the dark side of the food industry and Bob Dylan, who managed to eluded the trappings of celebrity and remain himself and last but certainly not least, Richard Branson for his belief in people and their innate positivity.

Apart from one or two of the characters on my list, under closer inspection you would probably discover that none of them are perfect, in fact, in some cases, far from it. I'm sure all of them have their bad habits and their odd weak moments and are very human when viewed in that way. However, we seem to forgive that, as we know at a deeper level, that something more important, powerful and sustaining is at play, something that causes us to forgive or overlook their all too human frailties.

There are a number of characteristics and traits that make our heroes and heroines outstanding. Without doubt though, they all seem to have two particular hallmarks in common. These qualities act like organizing principles and seem to be the collective source of some of their super-human levels of courage, persistence, strength, belief or wisdom.

These qualities are not just the exclusive domain of these special individuals. We all have access to them and possess the same ability to tap into them . We have all seen or know of people who have done this from time to time. I'm sure each of us can recall proud moments in our lives when we have momentarily became our own super-heroes, times when we pushed through our own limitations and fears and fleetingly touched the extra-ordinary.

Hallmark one: How big is your world?

We are all conditioned, if not genetically designed from birth, to fight our own corner. It's instinctual. We have that instinct, animals have it. If ever we get backed into a corner, we fight, even if that fight takes the form of talking our way out of something or feigning weakness. They are all the many forms of protecting ourselves and fighting our corner.

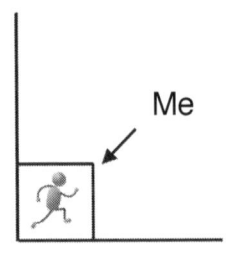

```
        ┌─────────────
        │
        │         Me
        │    ┌──┐ ↙
        │    │🏃│
        │    └──┘
        └────────────
```

This instinct lies deeply embedded within our limbic and ancient reptilian brains. This natural inborn tendency has allowed us to survive as a species and is a profoundly trusted set of urges and behaviours. It's what has got us here and we are very, very good at it. This is a deep and powerful instinct. However, I have noticed that if I'm acting on behalf of myself and myself alone, I can only access a small percentage of that power. Only a small amount of courage, wisdom, integrity and other finer qualities are made available to me.

Let us consider some everyday examples. Imagine I am on my own at home. It's 2 a.m. in the morning and I wake up to hear what sounds like a couple of intruders downstairs. If I'm on my own, I'll probably be thinking about where to hide or how to disappear myself. I'll certainly be wishing I had other family or friends in the house.

Now consider this: let's say I'm in my house and the same thing happens. It's 2 a.m. and there seems to be a couple of intruders downstairs in my house. The difference this time is that both my wife and son are in the house as well. I'm no longer thinking about where I'm going to hide or how I'm going to disappear myself. I'm now putting my underpants over my PJs and I'm Clark Kent become Superman. Suddenly, I can now access a whole new level of courage I wasn't able to before. I'm no longer just defending myself, I'm now protecting my family.

Family

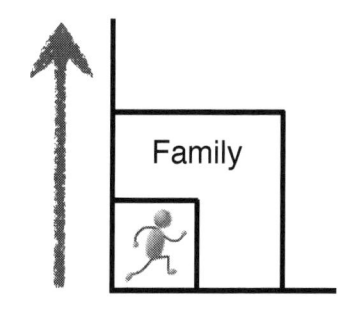

My corner just got bigger, much bigger. That's just the start. If I were to extend my corner further, there are many levels I could extend out to. Who is next closest to me after my immediate family? My friends. Who is next closest after my friends? My colleagues. And after that? My boss. Sometimes these categories blur. Sometime some of my friends also happen to be colleagues. We could keep going, extending our corner further and further out. You could also have finer distinctions if you wish, like after friends could come the category acquaintances for example. It's up to you, but I think you get the general gist.

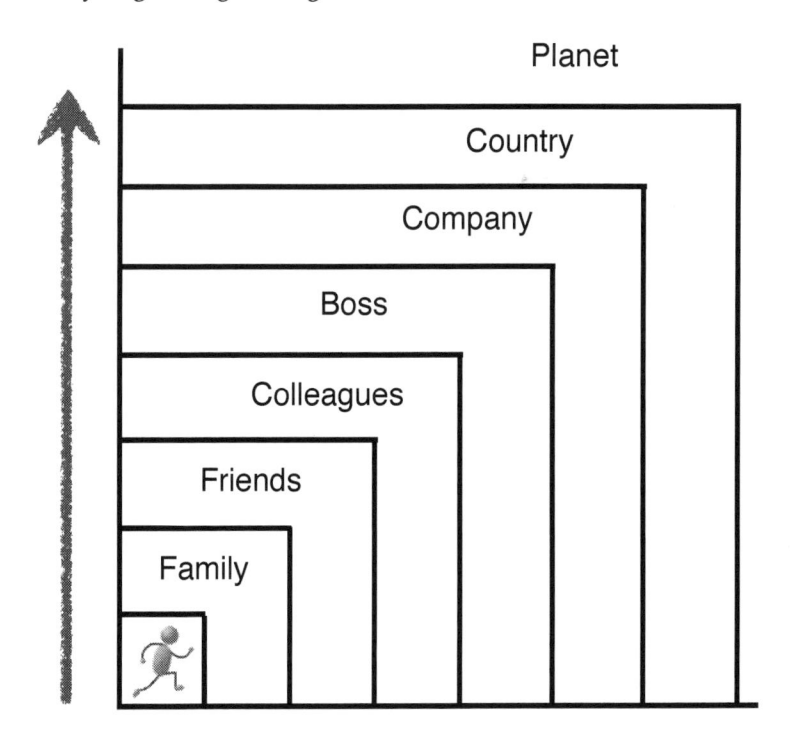

Planet
Country
Company
Boss
Colleagues
Friends
Family

The further I extend my corner, the greater access I have to courage, wisdom and all those other magical qualities we were discussing earlier. Let's take another example. This is not so much about courage, but more about the standards and level of quality we express. Let's say I am on my own and I'm feeling hungry. What do I do? Well, I'll probably chuck a ready meal into the microwave and count down the seconds. I'll use one utensil and a plate. If I'm in a bit of a hurry, I might even stand up whilst I'm eating the meal.

However, let's say it's lunch-time and Harrison and Sylvie are in the house. I may still put a couple of meals in the microwave, but I'll also knock up a bit of salad or cook some vegetables. I'll put out both knives and forks this time and we'll definitely be sitting down around the kitchen table.

But let's say some friends are coming around for a meal, what happens then? Well, we are now talking about a starter, as well as a main course and possibly even a dessert. Knives, forks and spoons are now involved and you might even see a candle or two and a bottle of wine may also make its way on to the table.

What if some colleagues are coming around for dinner? Well, we are now moving into a special room, the dining room. The best crockery comes out, napkins make an appearance, name-place cards are written and not only does the room get thoroughly cleaned and smartened up, but now Sylvie insists the whole house gets cleaned and dusted.

If the boss and their partner were coming over, some people might even go completely over the top and get a caterer in. The further out you go and the bigger your corner gets, the higher the standards and the greater access you get to those qualities we mentioned before.
I mentioned earlier that my grandfather used to tell his story of the second world war and the amazing manners and camaraderie people afforded each other. During that terrible period of time, amazing acts of bravery were witnessed. People would run in the direction that the bullets were coming from. You would only do that if you were fighting on behalf of something much bigger than yourself.

You can always tell how big someones corner is by where they draw their line between 'us and them'. Most teenagers draw that line between themselves and their parents. Most teenagers for example don't have the word 'Welcome' written lovingly on their door.

Family | Us and Them!

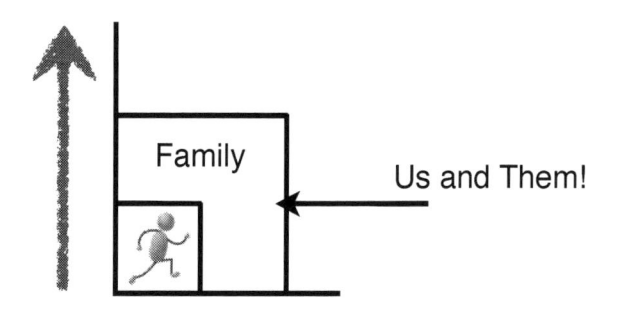

What I have just related was one of my favourite stories told by Woody. I think it brilliantly sums up the dynamic that allows some people to access so much more courage, integrity and stamina than most. The good news is that we all possess those qualities and can access them if we enlarge the size of our own corner.

Similar lines are often drawn at work. In many cases, the lines are often drawn between staff and management or staff and the executive. The size of your corner relates very strongly to Engagement. The greater the disengagement, the firmer the lines are drawn and the deeper the entrenched positions become. It becomes increasingly difficult to generate any sense of collective purpose or direction. The very worst thing is to have a senior manager or executive who is only in it for themselves. The team becomes a reflection of its leader. If they have a small corner, so will the team. Purpose, mission and 'going the extra mile' will be well off the menu.

Our great personal heroes are not in it for themselves. They are in it for something far greater. They operate, think, act, create and give consideration to things at a higher level. Their corner, or in other words, what they are willing to fight for, is much larger. You will usually find them conducting themselves at a country, planet or spiritual level. This is where they draw their inspiration, energy and ideas from.

If you look closely or do a bit of research, you will notice many people that work at the very top of their organisations are not necessarily the most highly qualified, possess the very brightest intellects or have the greatest longevity within the business. What they do have, is a big corner.

'The most inspiring individuals don't do things on behalf of themselves. They do it for something bigger than themselves. That is why we unconsciously respond so positively to them.'

To an extent, the ego is sacrificed and replaced by a bigger purpose. All heroes do that.

Parents do this quite naturally. Those of you who have kids or are around people that have kids, know this instinctively. When a child is born, something happens. Suddenly, it's no longer about you. Your corner just got bigger. Your corner now includes them and you will do whatever it takes to make their life great, even if that means some sacrifice. Mums and dads are heroes too!

If Mahatma Gandhi wanted a nice house and a successful law practice, he could have got that by keeping his head down, staying out of trouble and carrying on with his legal career. No need for lengthy incarcerations, physical punishment and self-imposed hunger strikes. He decided to put his own needs to one side and lived at a much higher level.

Some people who operate at the highest levels seem to receive great wisdom or have access to greater sagacity that others. Albert Einstein is just such one. He is often quoted as saying a number of things. One of the most commonly cited is 'Insanity is doing the same thing over and over again and expecting a different result'. It's a great quote. Personally, I prefer this quote: 'No problem can be solved from the same level of consciousness that created it.' In a way, it relates very strongly to the principle of 'How big is your corner?' and moving out to a higher level.

Bert always created a strong sense that he was doing what he was doing on behalf of something greater than himself. That's what made it so easy for those of us that worked with him, to accept him as our leader and give him all our backing.

As Viktor Frankl the eminent psychologist so eloquently put it, "Don't aim at success. The more you aim at it and make it a target, the more you are going to miss it. For success, like happiness, cannot be pursued, it must ensue, and it only does so as the unintended side-effect of one's personal dedication to a cause greater than one's self." So think bigger, go beyond yourself. Be a part of something greater than yourself. Some people take an active role in their community, some derive a great satisfaction and connection with their faith or family, some get involved with causes they resonate with, and others find passion in their work. In each case, the outcome is the same. They engage themselves in something they strongly believe in. It is the act of engagement that brings happiness, success, and meaning, not necessarily the thing in itself.

How big is your corner?
Where do you draw the line between Us and Them?
Would you be willing to consider increasing the size of your corner?

A great example of increasing the size of your corner happened in 1962. John F. Kennedy announced that his country was going to put a man on the moon, within the decade. One of the more popular fables to come out of that episode was during a visit of his to the NASA space centre. The President noticed a janitor carrying a broom. He interrupted his tour, walked over to the man and said, 'Hi, I'm Jack Kennedy. What are you doing?' 'Well, Mr. President,' the janitor responded, 'I'm helping put a man on the moon.'

That's a lovely story of true alignment and the power of a vision. I'm sure we've all heard it before and have been equally inspired by it. What is lesser known but probably more powerful, is that not only were all the distinguished scientists who supported the vision invited to join the team, but also invited were all those that were sceptical of its success and could see all the impossible barriers that couldn't be overcome? The leadership's corner was so big, it included both the believers and the sceptics. In fact, without the sceptics, how would you know what barriers and blocks needed to be overcome. That's the sort of wisdom and courage that comes from having a super-sized corner.

This would answer why we respond so positively to acts of selflessness; people that are doing something on behalf of something greater than themselves or simple acts of kindness. In equal measure, it is why we are so wary of selfish ambition, arrogance and vanity.

Hallmark two: The question you live in?

Of all the six questions in the English language, there is one question that holds the most power and the most potency. It's the question we soon learnt as kids that our parents seemed to struggle with the most and certainly the question they often failed to provide a decent answer to.

You're probably beginning to guess which question I mean. The question in question of course is WHY.

A 'Why' upgrade

Earlier in this book we started to explore a very interesting and telling question; 'Are you willing to consider doing a motive upgrade on the people in your lives?'

I'd like us to now consider taking this to the next level.

Are you willing to upgrade your Why?

I remember vividly when I first saw Simon Sinek's TED Talk in the latter part of 2009. It was called 'How great leaders inspire action'. It really was a stand out moment for me and confirmed many of my beliefs and ideas about the source of motivation, decision making and leadership itself. In fact, I was so impressed, I have shown it to many hundreds of people since.

He starts out with the question 'Why is Apple so innovative? Why is it that Martin Luther King led the civil rights movement?' and 'Why is it that the Wright Brothers were able to figure out controlled power manned flight?' He answers this by describing something he calls the Golden Circle

Why - It's why the business exists, its purpose.
How - How the company differentiates itself, its unique selling point
What - This is what the company does

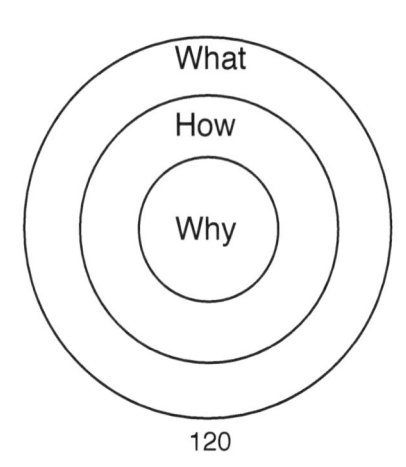

I'm sure many of you have seen the TED Talk. If you haven't seen it, I strongly suggest you do, it's one of the best out there. I have listed the website in the resource section of this book.

According to Simon Sinek, the fundamental difference between the "Apples" of the world and everyone else, is that they start with their 'why' and work their way out to 'what'.

He discovered that most companies do their marketing and communications the other way around; they do it backwards. They start with 'what they do' and then move on to 'how they do it'. More importantly, the majority of these companies neglect to even mention 'why' they do what they do. Closer to the truth, many of these organisations don't even know 'why' they do what they do (other than make a profit). To help illustrate this point, Simon Sinek goes on to say 'imagine if Apple, like many other organisations, also started backwards by creating a marketing message that started with their 'what'. It would go something like this'.

'We make great computers [What]. They're user-friendly, beautifully designed, and easy-to-use [How]. Want to buy one?' While these facts are true, I'm not sold, they are uninspiring. Here's what a real marketing message from Apple might actually sound like:

'With everything we do, we aim to challenge the status quo. We aim to think differently. Our products are user-friendly, beautifully designed, and easy-to-use. We just happen to make great computers. Want to buy one?'

See how different that feels? Because Apple starts with 'why' when defining their company, they are able to attract customers who share their fundamental beliefs. As Sinek puts it so well, 'People don't buy what you do. They buy **why** you do it.'

When an organisation articulates their WHY and we believe it, then we go above and beyond to include their offerings in our lives. We embrace their beliefs, not because they're necessarily better, but because they represent values that are important to us. They make us feel like we belong and these organisations are the ones that create loyal fan bases and brand ambassadors.

Great leaders, in any walk of life, have a clear 'why' and this is the reason they are able to appeal so powerfully at an emotional and heartfelt level. In simple terms, 'what you do' and the 'how you do it' is understood by the logical, neocortex. The 'why we do' what we do directly affects the limbic brain and stirs emotions, passions and ultimately decisions.

Great leaders have a great why. What's yours?

What is your 'Why'?

At this point, many of us hit a bit of a wall, or a blank. Most of us don't have much of a clear idea about what we want to do with our lives. It's a struggle almost every adult goes through. 'What do I want to do with my life?' Some of us just give up early and get cynical about the whole idea. Quite understandable. I believe one of the roots to this thorny problem is the very concept of 'my life's purpose' itself. The idea that we were each born for some specific hidden purpose and it's now our Herculean mission to find it. It's almost as if an inability to find this hidden artifact is, in some way, a mark of failure and a clear sign we are not one of the chosen ones. To make matters worse, now that 'having a life's purpose' has entered the popular mainstream, there are thousands of people professing to be clear and testifying how it has transformed their lives. That just makes the rest of us mere mortals feel a little more inadequate and it may even precipitate a small dose of 'purpose envy!' It all sounds terribly, terribly tiring. I'm not surprised some of us give up at this point. If like most people, a clear mission or vision doesn't appear before you in some sudden flash of inspiration or insight, start with something small, some thing you can do. The most important word in that sentence is 'start'. You could spend a whole lifetime searching for your ultimate purpose and actually end up doing nothing, other than just searching.

There are loads of excellent books, articles and blogs on the subject. The web is literally heaving with good ideas. Don't spend weeks trawling through endless pages trying to find the ultimate list. The real value starts with starting. There are some really good questions you could pose yourself and they will certainly help throw some light on your 'Why'. You will see some or all of these on most lists that are out there. All you have to do is type in 'Questions to help you find your life's purpose'. Click search and you'll get pages of the stuff; good stuff too.

- What would I do if I knew I couldn't fail?
- What do I want to be remembered for?

- What am I most proud of and what values were I expressing at that time?
- Who are my heroes and what do I admire in them?
- What would I do if money was no object?

Personally, I'd rather start with something smaller and closer to home, something I can really get on with. I had a good look at the people around me and started to look a bit more closely at those people that I experienced really had something about them, something I admired or something that caught my attention in some way.

I started to realize that what I value or regard highly in others, are the very same values I possess within myself. This might sound an obvious thing, but to me it wasn't at the time. I just thought they had something I wanted, but didn't have at the moment. When I admire something in someone, whether it be what they do or how they go about doing it, it's my own same values, in myself, that are resonating. I have what they have, but my volume knob is at a lower setting, so it seems I don't have it at all. That's not true. I just need to crank it up.

I learnt a simple trick and it's the simplest and oldest trick of them all.

COPY IT

We are born with this facility. It's how we learnt to eat, to talk, to walk, and relate. For some reason however, beyond a certain age our ego takes over and decides: 'I'm going to do it my way'. From that point on, copying becomes uncool. I had a not-so-wonderful introduction to this idea in my early 20's

In the chapter 'The Language of Engagement', I told the story of how I left my humdrum job at the drum business and how I had joined this amazing band of brothers at the telephone marketing company. The story doesn't stop there. If anything, the journey had just begun.

In the first few days, I and about ten other equally excited recruits went through an intensive induction training, the likes of which I had never seen or experienced before. We spent hour upon hour just doing listening drills, we practiced using just the intention in our voice to make someone say 'yes' back to us. There was even a session where we were pushing a wall as hard we could, as if our life depended on it, as a symbol of our willingness to push through our personal barriers to success. I don't think you could get away with some of that stuff today. Crazy, but really quite brilliant.

The following Monday, we were to start on our first project. Our client was a well-known computer company and the task was to set appointments for their sales executives to meet relevant financial directors.

As you can imagine, I was extremely nervous. I stuttered so badly on the first call that the customer had to finish my sentences. Towards the end of the week, it was becoming clear that my results were poor and below the required standard. This was proving a lot harder than I had anticipated.

On the Friday, my team leader, Annabel, pulled me to one side before the start of the morning session. Annabel has about the steeliest determination in her eyes you are ever likely to come across on planet Earth, maybe beyond too. Not only that, she was utterly direct and disarmingly truthful. She said in her inimitable way 'David you are failing. Your way is not working. Jan (the female sales goddess sat opposite me) is achieving three times better results than you are. I want you to sit next to her and copy exactly what she does'. Jan's style couldn't be more different than mine, I was horrified. 'But Jan's different to me, I'm not like her at all' I reasoned. 'You bet Jan's different to you. She's three times better than you. If you don't copy her and improve your results, I'm going to invite you to leave'. I was shocked. My ego was insulted and the thought of copying Jan's larger-than-life style was a nightmare. However, copy it I did.

I never managed to quite eclipse the results of Jan, she really was and still is a one-off, but boy were my sales getting better. It didn't take me too long to realise that there were also a few other people there that we getting pretty good results too. I made it my business to sit next to them and tried to glean some of their top tips as well. After about three months, I had crafted a style that was really working.

That was an amazing lesson for me and a road I would never have gone down were it not for the lovely Annabel. I learnt to let go of trying to do it my way and put far more attention on finding who and what the best were doing and copy that. My ego didn't like it at first, but it soon got the hang of it, especially when people were now asking me how I was getting such great results. I felt like a hero. In truth, I had broken through to a completely new level of ability, not by being brilliant, but by getting myself out of the way and doing what others were doing better.

'Talent is the ability to copy'

I'm not suggesting you adopt the Annabel-style of management. That was reserved for a different time and a different place. In fact, I recommend you don't. You would find yourself being asked to leave pretty Rapido! The point is though, I'm sure you could find a way of delivering the exact same learning in a manner appropriate to todays environment.

On reflection, what I also realized prior to Annabel's lesson, what I called 'my way', was simply a collection of stuff I had learnt (copied) previously from the people around me when I was much younger. I'm sure as adults, we sometimes catch ourselves out using the same phrases or expressions as our parents. You will particularly notice this if you have brought up kids. Have you ever watched a parent and their son or daughter together, engrossed in something and oblivious of anything else around them? You'll suddenly see the same expressions, gestures and mannerisms. It's quite a thing to see.

All I am doing now is being far more selective about what and who I am copying. If your ego doesn't like the word copy, try emulate or model. It's more palatable, but essentially the same thing.

If you delve into the world of sports and see interviews of some of the outstanding sportsmen and sportswomen of our time, they will all tell the same story of how they spent year upon year trying to emulate their heros. For Wayne Rooney it was Francis Jeffers, for Usain Bolt it was Muhammad Ali, Michael Jordan and Michael Johnson, for Pele it was his father. Pele observed his father João play soccer for hours on end, hoping that someday he would become a professional player himself. Well, that certainly happened.

As a kid of twelve, mucking about with my mates playing football, we didn't call ourselves by our real names; David, Andy, Geoff and John, we called ourselves by our football hero's names. I was usually in goal, so I was 'Bonetti the Cat' (of Chelsea fame).

I'm not saying all you have to do is pretend to be Pele for ten years and you'll be a world-class footballer, but you might be surprised how far it takes you down that road.

This lesson is not confined to sales. Far from it.

I'm a great believer in standing on the shoulders of giants and not reinventing the wheel. If someone is doing something really well or seems to be making a real difference, or I just simply like the way they do something, I copy it.

As I said earlier in this chapter, personally, I would rather start with something smaller and closer to home, something I can really get on with. Gradually I realized, right in front of me, there was more than enough genius to be getting on with. If I resonate strongly to someone's 'why', I absorb it and make it mine. I wasn't born with a still, clear voice in my head telling me what my purpose in life was, so I copied the best I could find and made them mine. It's worked a treat.

As you can no doubt tell, I allowed Bert to have a significant influence on my management style. His unswerving ability to remember everyone is an A, to maintain positive labels and preserve his positive motive was an inspiration.

My wife Sylvie was bought up behind the Iron Curtain and learnt how to have the most possible fun imaginable with very little material wealth. Absorbing her gift has led me back to the pure delight of simple pleasures, far removed from my prior materialistic pursuit of bigger, better, faster, stronger.

Woody's uncompromisingly optimistic, loving outlook and his unshakeable belief that everyone has positive intent (if you just bothered to understand the whole story) has transformed any remnants of cynicism I might have had left in me.

These are just a few snippets of some of my own examples. You will have loads of your own. When it comes to clarifying your own 'why', certainly work on the bigger stuff, but the main thing is to start somewhere. I prefer to start with what's around me and build out from there.

It's very hard to maintain a sense of purpose and stay engaged if you boss doesn't have one. If you don't have one, get one.

Clean relationships

A clean relationship is one where we are fully up to date and there is nothing incomplete or anything out there that needs to be said to clear the air. It's fantastic working with a team where we have clean relationships and co-operation comes as naturally as breathing.

A lot of companies are trying to upgrade the level of co-operation and collaboration within their businesses, because they instinctively feel that greater co-operation would unlock significant potential.

I would agree with that sentiment. I have certainly seen many situations where a bit more co-operation, collaboration and just being joined-up would release many tangible benefits.

Co-operation is not the thing to target however, clean relationships are. A lack of co-operation or collaboration however are just symptoms of something far more causative. Earlier we were looking at rapport and we explored a simple consequence of cause and effect. 'Where there is no rapport, there are politics. A similar causal relationship exists between co-operation and clean relationships'

'Where there are no clean relationships there will be obstruction'

Co-operation is the natural state between people. You don't have to create it. What you do have to do is ensure the right conditions are in place to support it. The primary condition is 'Clean Relationships'. As with any natural state, it arises quite naturally when the conditions are right. It's not so different from growing potatoes. As long as the soil is good, the sun shines and there is rain from time to time, they will pop up of their own accord. You can't convince a potato it has to grow. It does it when the conditions are right. They don't even have to be perfect, potatoes just need the basics and they get on with the business of growing. Co-operation doesn't require perfect conditions either, it just needs some of the right basics in place.

At this point, it would be tempting to prescribe some stock formulae for building 'clean relationships'. All you have to do is follow the trusted recipe and voilà, problem sorted. Of course, in real life, this notion doesn't pan out like that and often falls flat on its face. I recommend you increase your awareness of the state of the relationships of the people that work with you and around you. In particular, get as sensitized as you can to 'incompletions'.

Amongst many insightful things, Simon Sinek quoted a very useful phrase. 'Leaders are called leaders because they go first'. If you want to enjoy the benefits that arise out of clean relationships; co-operation, collaboration and greater engagement, BE-ing the change you want to create is essential.

In my early twenties, I was introduced to an idea that put me far more firmly in the driving seat of my life. I am very grateful for it, as it certainly changed the course of my life and the story of how David Coleman was likely to unfold. The idea consisted of three little words. These little words are surprisingly powerful. They became my guiding north star when it came to transforming or upgrading my own experience and the circumstances around me.

BE - DO - HAVE

Many people tend to approach things from the other end, the other way around:

HAVE - DO - BE

Confidence is a good example of this. I used to think: 'when I feel confident, I will do things that confident people do and then I will have confidence'. I was waiting to feel confident before I did things that required it. Naturally, I would wait for long periods of time for this feeling to turn up! When it came to money, I used to think in a similar manner: 'when I get a million pounds, then I'll be a millionaire; when I get the Ferrari, then I'll be successful; when I get the perfect relationship, then I'll be happy'. It's the sort of thinking that leads to that old trap of constantly requiring bigger, better, faster, stronger, stuff to feel satisfied.

It was suggested to me that it actually works the other way around. I didn't realize at the time that I had adopted an unconscious victim position. My circumstances, my possessions, my bank balance and the state of my relationships, all determined the happiness levels in my life.

When I re-arranged the order of the three little words, it profoundly repositioned me from being the victim of my circumstances and events, to one where I was the driver of my train, rather than a passenger sat within it.

All over the planet, there are people in meetings, writing up lists of things to do differently, to improve efficiency, productivity, customer experience, staff turnover and all manner of things. We are all good at lists. Millions of sheets of flip-chart paper, white boards, PowerPoint pages and backs of fag packets have been pressed into service for these purposes. We love lists.

Like any list, some of the actions are easy and some not so. We are very familiar with this and all have our own strategies for managing them. Some put off the harder ones for later, some develop elaborate reasons why some items couldn't be completed, some go for the hard ones first, we all have our ways. A lot of this boils down to our relationship with our comfort zone. Items that lie within our zone are easy and often get done first. Items that lie outside of our zone however, are an entirely different kettle of fish. Ideas that may take us outside of our comfort zone stimulate emotion and wake up the limbic mind, a bit like the Harry Potter three-headed sleeping dog. Not much gets passed the three-headed dog. One eye is always half open, even in the deepest of slumbers.

Comfort zones

Our comfort zones simply describe those things we feel comfortable doing. Each of us have different comfort zone. Some feel comfortable on a motorbike, others back off from a ride if it's offered. Some feel comfortable going up to strangers and introducing themselves, whilst others prefer to be approached, rather than make the first move. Some feel comfortable with new technology whereas others prefer the feel of pen and paper. And the list goes on. I think one thing most of us will agree on though, is that right in the middle of our comfort zones is a nice big soft, comfortable bed.

Let's look at some examples to explain this in more detail. Imagine I'm a Team Leader at a contact centre. My company is a large mobile network operator. Apple have just bought out their latest iPhone and the number of people wanting to upgrade has significantly exceeded our forecast. The centre can't handle the volume of calls at all and the queue of customers trying to get through is relentless. I'm sure you can imagine this, both from a customer and employee perspective. All-round frustration. On top of that, I've now been persuaded to do more overtime than I wanted and all training and non-core activities have been suspended indefinitely. There I am at 9.15 a.m. in our monthly briefing session on the Monday morning. Without announcement and mid sentence, the door to the meeting room flies open and in walks the CEO. This is my boss's, boss's, boss's boss. He reaches the front of the room, turns to face us, smiles benignly and begins to speak. *'I know all of you have been under immense pressure over the last period. In a way you could say we've been victims of our own success. I know that we are not out of the woods yet by any means, but I just felt I had to speak to you and thank you for your heroic efforts so far. I've been really impressed with your positive attitude and willingness to turn up every day to deal with this tidal wave of interest. Whilst I cannot offer you any guarantees, our best estimates indicate that we should be able to return to normal business levels within the next six to seven weeks. We'll keep you updated with this, as and when we can. The good news is, through the hard work you and your colleagues have been doing, we have managed to help a record number of customers to switch to our service. I'm very pleased and full of admiration for what you have all achieved. Well done to each of you, particularly given the critical roles you play'.*

'Whilst we've broken some records, there are some other records we need to address as well. During this period, due to our elevated call volumes, we haven't managed to speak to some of the customers trying to contact us. Some of them understandably are not very happy at all. I have personally received more letters of complaint in the last couple of months that we did for the entirety of last year'.

'In response to that, I have invited our top three hundred most upset customers to a central London hotel and we are going to use it as an opportunity to apologize, give them a great day out and hopefully win them back. I'm very much looking forward to it, I think it's going to be a great event. The lunch menu looks superb and in the afternoon, we've got some very interesting fun and games lined up. I think they'll really enjoy it. In the morning however, there is the serious business of listening to the complaints from the floor and responding to them 'live' in front of the

audience of three hundred. Now normally, myself or one of my fellow directors would run this session, as it's potentially very tricky. But I thought: 'no, let's keep this real and get one of our people who have actually being handling the complaints, to run this session'. I'm pleased to announce, based on the highest conversion rate, that DAVID COLEMAN has been selected to run this session. Congratulations! The 'Customer Day' is in three weeks time, so you have ample time to prepare and get yourself ready. Don't worry, there's no need to feel nervous, as I and the full board of directors will be at the back of the room to help, if you get into trouble.'

Up until my name was mentioned, I was just enjoying the praise from the privacy and comfort of my own mind, as if watching TV. Suddenly I've been shocked out of my cosy reality and I'm very, very present and catapulted way outside of my comfort zone! I'm not doing the talk yet, but in just imagining it, I'm already starting to leave my zone.

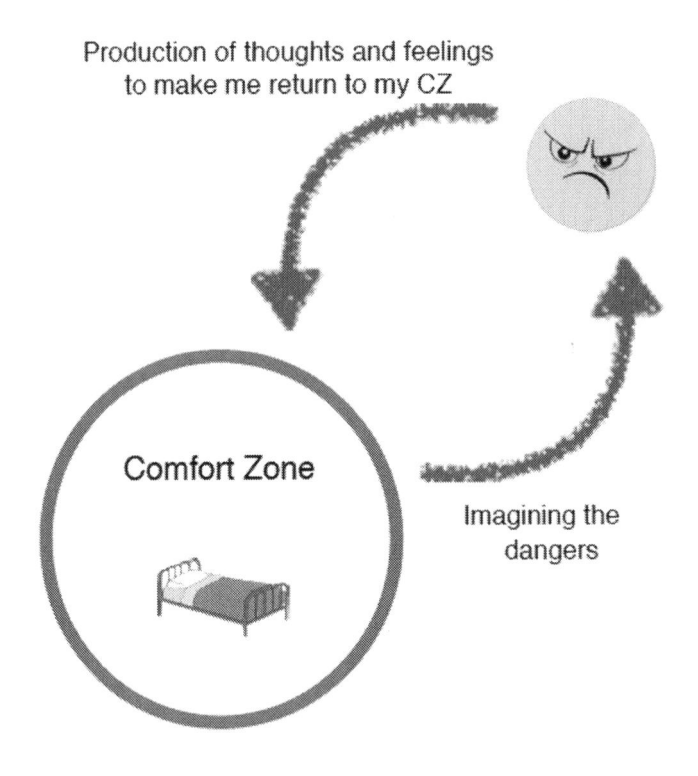

Production of thoughts and feelings to make me return to my CZ

Comfort Zone

Imagining the dangers

How can you tell if you are leaving your comfort zone? What are the symptoms? The very first thing you notice is that you start to have feelings and body sensations. In my case it was sweaty palms, butterflies in my stomach, hardly breathing, increased heart rate and my mind started spinning.

This is the classic 'fight and flight' response and a clear sign I have just ventured outside of my comfort zone. The job of survival, as I'm sure you have already guessed, is very much the domain of the Limbic brain. What has happened is our Limbic brain has calculated that we are potentially about to encounter danger and pulls the adrenaline lever. Hard.

This 'fight and flight' response has been with us for eons. We inherited it from our primate ancestors and they from their ancestors in turn. It has proved over time, to be a very successful response to danger. So useful in fact, that it has been retained and preserved very carefully and is hardwired as our primary response to any form real or imagined danger. In my example, I am in no physical danger. I am sat in a comfortable chair, supported two feet about the floor. I am in no physical danger at all, yet my body is responding as if there is a lion or some other predator in the room.

The CEO is certainly not a predator. However, when he has ideas like that, for me, he certainly feels like one. My imagination gets to work on his kind offer of standing up in front of three hundred angry people and dreams up all sorts of potential scenarios of things that can go wrong.

You could argue that our limbic mind is now over-stepping its brief. Not only is it protecting us from real physical danger, it has now increased its remit to include our precious egos and the 'image' we have of ourselves. For this reason, not only are we afraid of real physical dangers, but we are now also afraid of imaginary and non-life threatening fears as well. Unfortunately, the better your imagination, the more you can dream up to be afraid or worried about. Sometimes, having a good imagination is not necessarily an advantage!!

Primary non-life-threatening fears

Failure
Rejection
Disapproval or not being liked or accepted
Embarrassment
Humiliation
Loss of control
Loss of status or position
Being misunderstood
Revenge or consequences
Letting people down

The limbic mind equates leaving our comfort zone with danger and potential mortality.

Its job is to ensure you return to your comfort zone.
What will set you apart is your ability to distinguish between real and imagined danger and the difference between authentic survival and self-limiting 'over survival'

To make double-sure we return to our comfort zone, not only are we delivered a sharp dose of uncomfortable body sensations (which we call fear), we are also fed a number of ideas that either help us or convince us to return to the safety of our comfort zone. Let us call these 'Survival Thoughts'.
The survival thoughts we are given, either designed to help us or convince us to return to our comfort zone, tend to take three forms.

A direct instruction
An excuse
A reason

A direct instruction can be simple things like 'run', 'hide', 'freeze', 'fight'. These are very instinctive and we are very familiar with them. They don't happen often, but when they do we don't argue with them. These instructions are issued when we are in very real physical danger.

We are also very familiar with the second form of 'survival thoughts': excuses. Excuses are designed to help us avoid things that are usually in the 'imagined threat' category. They are often manufactured 'white lies' or 'convenient truths'. Their main purpose though, is to get out of the situation which we believe may cause us discomfort or worse.

In the case of my standing up in front of three hundred people, I will definitely be trying to come up with one or two excuses. The trouble is: I can't be seen to be just trying to wiggle out of it by the CEO. That could be a career-limiting move. Somehow I have to use my advanced sucking up skills, yet still manage to get out of it. So I might say,

'I'm really honoured that you have invited me and I feel very proud to be able to represent this group and the company as a whole. Unfortunately, my holiday is on that date and I simply can't get out of it. However, Mandy is very good at this sort of thing…if you want, I'd be happy to brief her and make sure the whole event works brilliantly. I'll also liaise with the hotel to ensure the room is well set up. Yes, so I'll get on with that then!'

Effectively, all I've done is got out of it. I'm sure we've all done something along those lines before. Excuses are pretty easy to notice in others and ourselves. The really tricky ones are REASONS. Reasons are so well-constructed and logical that even we get sucked into their validity.

The number of opportunities I have turned down or talked myself out of because of the 'reasons' I put in their way, just doesn't bear thinking about. For example. In my late twenties I increasingly began to want to set up my own business and go it alone. I would often tell my wife and would get excited when imagining the possibilities that stretched out before me. Eventually, I set myself a date for when I would leave my existing employer and set out as a brave young entrepreneur. The closer the date came, the more I started to feel uncomfortable. The more uncomfortable I got, the fuller my head became with reasons why perhaps this was not such a good idea. Often these thoughts would arrive in the form of questions.

'What if it doesn't work?'
'They won't have you back…Then what will you do?'
'Is now really the right time to be doing this, especially now your wife is pregnant?'

It didn't take long for these 'survival thoughts' to do their evil work and force me to loosen my grip on my dreams. Fortunately, I had been made aware of this self-limiting process and I was able to see these 'survival thoughts' for what they really were.

One of the greatest lessons I learned on this subject came by the way of an amazing woman. She was running the contact centre I spoke about earlier in the book. This lady was disarmingly powerful and insightful and had the unnerving ability to know what was going on with you, just by looking at you. I got on very well with her and always felt she held me in high regard and had a positive motive towards me.

One day, as a team leader I was managing my team and trying to hit our sales target. She approached me and invited me to come to her office at the beginning of my next break. I had no idea what it was about, perhaps a promotion or a salary increase. Who knows? I got to her office at the start of my lunch break. 'Thanks for coming' she said, 'I just want to let you know something, as it's something I think you ought to know'. She paused and looked at me in the way only this lady could, 'Whilst I run this business, you are never going to get into the senior management team. I just thought I'd let you know that just in case you thought you might want to. Anyway, have a good day and get those sales!'

I was temporarily speechless, not knowing whether to be furious, insulted or both. Not being particularly confident at that time, rather than telling her what I really thought, I enquired politely as to why she held that view.

'Oh, the answer to that is simple' she smiled 'It's because you're reasonable'. I just didn't get it, I didn't get it at all. I'd always considered being reasonable as an admirable quality. 'I'm sorry' I said, 'I just don't get it. You're going to have to spell it out for me'.

'The thing is this, David. Every time we've asked you to double your target or achieve something you think can't be done, you always come up with REASONS for why things can't be done. You are full of REASONS....You are REASON-able. As a REASON-able person you will never breakthrough and make something happen outside of your limitations. You will never make magic happen. I only want people in my senior team who can make magic happen. So, have a nice day and get those sales'.

That was, without doubt, one of the finest pieces of feedback I have ever received, although I have to admit, it was pretty painful at the time. I learnt how to distinguish the difference between real and imagined dangers; most importantly, I learnt how to spot a REASON at 100 yards, especially my own. Two years later, I was a member of that senior team, passing on the same lesson to someone else. She had obviously noticed I needed to overcome my issue with self-limiting 'REASONS' and was generous enough to help me step up to the next level.

Let's come back to my example of being offered the opportunity of hearing complaints from the three hundred angry customers. Let's say, in a moment of madness, I agreed to the task and was set to face my ordeal in three weeks time. I'd probably work with a colleague to try to imagine all the possible complaints the customers would come up with and all the possible ways we could answer them satisfactorily. I would also practice this over and over again, until I could handle questions at random and apply the appropriate responses. Of course, on the day, it's all different because my body is now full of adrenaline, my head is full of twenty different versions of how I might mess it up and I can't remember any of my rehearsed answers. I make my way to the table at the front of the room. It has a white table cloth and a microphone. I am joined by the CEO who makes the introduction, explains the purpose of the day and then withdraws to the back of the room, joining the assembled board, as promised. My heart is in my mouth. I can't really hear the first complaint, I saw their mouth moving but could make sense of the words. I apologize and politely ask them to repeat the question. I manage a poorly-formed response. Whilst answering some of the question, the customer is still shaking their head, as are some of her neighbours. Slowly, as the session continues I begin to recognize the questions more accurately and am able to respond with some well structured and informative responses. The audience can see me gaining in confidence and at some level, admire the courage it must be taking to be exposed to such a difficult crowd. Towards the end of the session, I'm really starting to nail some of my responses and the audience are even beginning to stare at one or two people that are clearly just moaning for the hell of it. I glance towards the back row. The CEO is beaming at me and nodding thankfully. His colleagues look equally relieved and pleased. I'm breathing again.

What do you imagine happens to my comfort zone? It expands! Maybe not all the way, but certainly the next time I get asked to do something similar, I won't be so put off by my feelings or 'survival thoughts'. Do that sort of thing enough times and before you know it, running a session like that becomes something you look forward to. It transforms from a nightmare into a challenge.

Conversely, turn down an opportunity like that a few times and your comfort zone starts to shrink. Each time it shrinks, you increase the distance between the edge of your comfort zone and the situation you are avoiding. It feels further away. The greater the distance, the stronger the feelings and the more convincing the 'survival thoughts'.

All of us have left our comfort zones many times. There is no way you would have the jobs you have, or would have done some of the things you have done, if you had not left your zone from time to time. Clearly, as well as the gravity of negative feelings and survival thoughts trying to pull us back into our comfort zones, there seems to be a force pushing us out. I call this force: 'Desire', or how much you 'want' to do things. If the gravity is greater than the 'desire to do something' then we decide not to do it and justify it with a reason or an excuse. If the 'desire' is greater than the gravity trying to pull us back, we decide to do it and as a consequence, our comfort zone expands.

The importance of desire

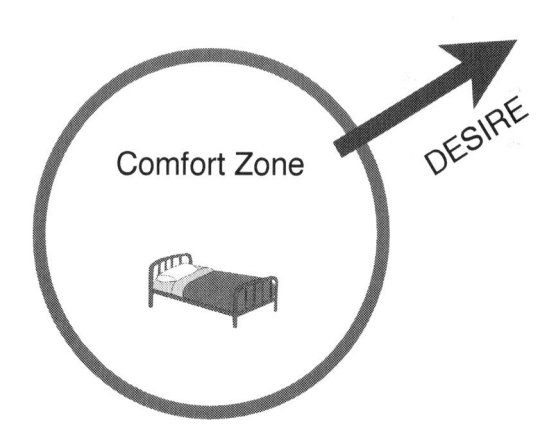

You can't stop the gravity of negative feelings and 'survival thoughts'. That's part of your hard-wiring. When those stop, it means you're dead!

What you can do though, is grow your desire. That's quite a life skill. Some people allow their desire or fire to be diminished down to a mere pilot-light. In some people, their fire is barely visible. When this happens, all that fire is replaced by reasons, opinions, moaning, stress and worry. Not good.

Other people have managed to keep that desire going and don't allow their 'over survival' to dampen their flames. When this happens, what you will see is someone with optimism, curiosity and a carefreeness born out of true confidence.

When considering comfort zones, the barrier we normally feel we have to push through is fear. There are four other primary barriers. Arrogance, anger, self-pity and apathy. Each of these barriers have associated 'survival thoughts', which manifest themselves whenever you hit one of these barriers.

Apathy is a very strong emotion and holds many with a vice-like grip. Let's say I have promised my wife that I will cut the grass before my parents come for lunch on the weekend. Two days before their arrival, she reminds me I haven't cut the grass: she invites me in no uncertain terms to get on with it. I'm not filled with fear at this point. I live in the UK, there is nothing dangerous in the grass that will leap out and bite me. I don't feel fear, but what I do feel is a tsunami of apathy descend on me. My body gets filled with the desire to procrastinate and put off the terrible event. I may even say

'Come on, it's only my parents, it's not as if the queen is coming' or a rather feeble 'what's the point, it will only grow back again'. I may even resort to a technical-based lie. 'The grass is wet, it dulls the blade!'. Apathy is characterised by 'what's the point', 'it doesn't matter', 'I'll do it tomorrow' and 'I really don't care'. It's a powerful emotion and can become a terrible habit and for some, a way of life. Interestingly, when I do actually get the mower out and start cutting the grass, I actually enjoy it.

'It's not cutting the grass that's the problem. It's the 'thinking about cutting it!' that's the problem'

Self pity, as the name suggests, is all about 'it's not fair', 'it always happens to me', 'when am I going to get a break', 'what about me', 'I'm not good enough', 'they are stopping me', 'they are making me feel this way'. Self-pity is designed to position the individual as a victim of their circumstances and limit their ability or desire to leave their comfort zone.

Fear, as discussed, is very much centred around thoughts such as 'I can't', 'what if it doesn't work', 'what will they think', 'it hasn't been done before'. Fear is a very powerful emotion, especially as it is so closely tied with our limbic survival strategies. Sometimes, it's really useful to get someone else's opinion on whether something is feasible or not. Just be careful about who you chose!

Anger is the emotion of 'I'm right, you're wrong' and often takes the form of unhelpful, repetitive thinking patterns. Language is sometimes distorted to increase the intensity of the emotion through the use of 'universal quantifiers': he NEVER considers my opinion: you ALWAYS interrupt me: she ALWAYS tells me what to do: I have to do ALL the work: I NEVER get a break: EVERYBODY picks on me.' Not held in check, anger can spill over into bullying, being over-critical and passive or even overt aggression.

Arrogance, or negative pride, is dominated by the feeling of 'how dare they?', 'do they have any idea of who I am?', 'I shouldn't have to do that', 'that is beneath me'.

It is a primary life skill of a successful leader to be able to identify 'survival thoughts' and recognize when they are hitting one of the five primary negative emotions. Leaders only go first if they are willing to leave their comfort zones and challenge their own 'reasonableness'.

Developing and maintaining 'clean relationships' frequently takes you outside of your comfort zone. That's why it's key to recognize these emotions and thoughts and to not argue yourself out of important conversations.

Be more courageous, be more curious, be more forgiving, be stronger, be more loving, be more happy, be more positive, be more open, be more kind, be more selfless.

Are you willing to consider upgrading your BE?

You always have a choice of how to BE, no matter what your circumstances. Some people with terrible setbacks choose to BE remarkable and do remarkable things. You don't have to look too far to see examples of that on a daily basis.

Choosing to ensure you are surrounded by people with 'clean relationships' will cause you to have a few conversations you weren't necessarily planning on having. But you know what, it's not that dissimilar to mowing the grass. At first, I'll find all the reasons not to do it, but once I'm actually out there cutting the grass, it feels great. You will probably find the people you speak to will love it. They may be a bit resistant at first, but everyone responds positively to higher standards. It's the basis of real pride.

Love	Honesty	Acceptance	Justice
Passion	Cooperation	Gratitude	Integrity
Joy	Wisdom	Trust	Modesty
Courage	Equality	Generousity	Creativity
Openness	Truth	Abundance	Grace
Peace	Happiness	Mercy	Optimism
Respect	Reliability	Giving	Understanding

Arrogance
Anger
Fear
Self pity
Apathy

Choose to live above the line. It will change you.

Short cycles

If you examine the historical sales records of many companies, particularly if they are selling large items or items of relatively high value, you will notice a little anomaly in the figures. Under closer examination, what you will see is a disproportionally higher value of sales being closed in December than in any other month of the year (or whichever month happens to be the last month of the trading year.)

This is often down to the simple human trait of procrastination: 'I've got loads of time, I'll focus on this later', 'I'll do it tomorrow'. This doesn't just apply to sales goals, it applies to anything from tax returns, keeping in contact with friends and family, cleaning the house, going to the dentist, apologizing or even telling someone you love them.

Short cycles is a simple rule that relates directly to the 'Great Circle'.

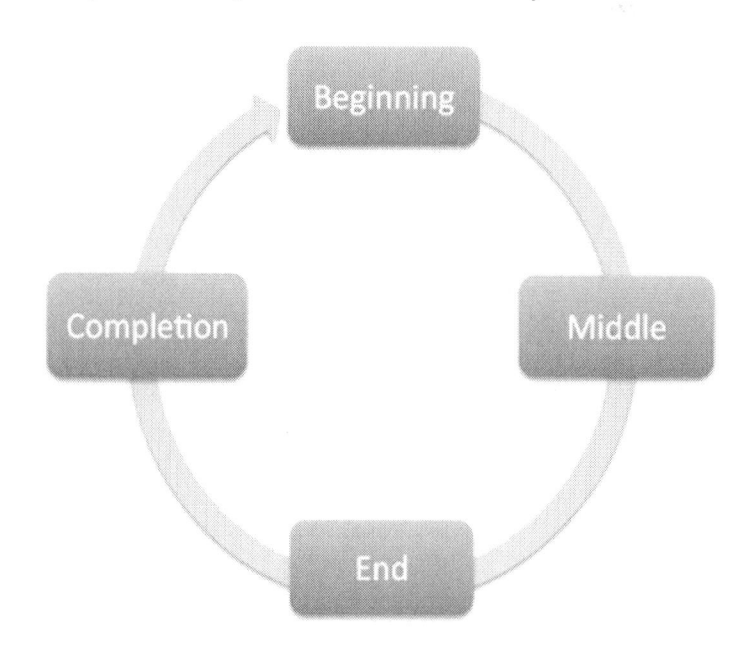

The shorter the cycle, the greater the engagement.

You could also argue, the shorter the cycle, the greater the energy as well. For example, in certain forms of the game, a cricket match is played over five days. It is associated with a certain level of energy and movement and often involves sandwiches, gin and tonic and the occasional snooze, should the passage of play become somewhat turgid. On completion of the five days, it is quite possible that there will be no result and end in a draw. In 135 years of Test Cricket (the five day format), to date, at the writing of this book, 2085 matches have been played, of which 35% were draws. By my calculation thats about 3649 days of waiting around for zero result. That's ten years! I feel I should reveal my hand at this point: cricket is my favourite team sport and it runs deep in my family. It's a good example of what I am talking about, though.

The Six Nations Championship is the oldest rugby championship in the world, dating back to 1882. It is played over just 80 minutes and, of all matches played to date, only about 4% have resulted in draws. If you were to film the audience watching the two games, cricket and rugby, you would see an entirely different scene at each of the games. In one, there would be occasional polite applause, scorecards being referred to, chatting and the occasional nodding off. In the other, you'd see bulging eyes, yells of encouragement, fierce eye-contact, watching every move and steam rising off large sections of the crowd. The difference in energy and engagement is stunning. What's even more telling is that many cricket fans are also rugby fans and they behave entirely differently, depending on what they are attending.

In 2003, a new form of the cricket game was created called Twenty20. Each side would have a very limited time to score their runs (20 overs) and then bowl the other side out. The game requires the players to take far more risk and play a more attacking and exciting style. The whole game is wrapped up in three hours and very rarely ends in a draw. This shorter, more energetic format of the game, has become very popular indeed. In fact, set against the growing popularity of Twenty20 cricket (particularly in India and Australia), there are serious concerns at the highest level of the game, that its most traditional format, the five day game, could die out. This is a good example of a sport introducing shorter cycles to increase engagement.

In a work scenario, if you see periods towards the end of the cycle, where productivity or efficiency increases, this is a sure sign that cycle-times could be usefully shortened.

Unfortunately, in today's busy world with the need to improve efficiency and maximize productivity, some of the very things that help to shorten cycle times and drive energy are the first things to suffer: frequency of goal-setting, huddles per day or week, debriefs, progress checks and milestone trackers.

If I think back to the time when I worked the hardest and with the most energy and enthusiasm, it was when I set targets twice a day and checked in with my progress at the end of each session. I was absolutely flying. I was 100% engaged and time seemed to speed up dramatically. As I got increasingly senior, a few things would happen: my chair got bigger, I got further and further away from customers and my goal cycles moved out to monthly or even annual cycles. In a funny way, I had more responsibility but was actually working at a slower rate. Of course, I wouldn't tell anyone that, but that's what seemed to be happening. I know there is a lot more to it than my simplistic explanation. The more senior your role, the more the nature of your goals change. Your remit is wider and some of the things you are now responsible for have appropriately longer time cycles. Having said that, these larger goals can be chunked down into smaller pieces and the same law applies. Shorter cycles create greater energy and engagement. As we said earlier, if you need to get something done, give it to a busy man. People that get things done tend to work off shorter cycles.

The notion of Shorter cycles can also work well for us in our personal lives, particularly when it comes to engagement. The more frequently I speak to my son, the more engaged I feel and the more I feel part of his life. The more frequently I participate in my hobby, photography, the more interested I get to be in it. The more time Sylvie and I spend just hanging out together, the closer we feel and the more alive our relationship.

It works the other way around too. How many friendships, I mean really good friendships, have withered due to the cycle of contact just being too long? How many relationships went stale because the cycle of thanking and appreciation slowed up? How many people got out of the gym habit because the frequency just wasn't high enough?

Leading from the front

Organisations are structured in such a way that the main idea seems to be to get away from the front-line and get as close to the top as you can. This is subconsciously sign-posted and incentivized financially, by role importance, by where the power seems to lie and by where decisions emanate from.

It could be argued that this might have the unfortunate effect of ensuring that all of your brightest and best are trying to migrate away from the most important part of the business, the various interfaces between the organisation and its customers.

In their excellent book 'The Spirit Level', professors Kate Pickett and Richard Wilkinson give us some very interesting facts. In 2007, chief executives of the 365 largest companies in the US received well over 500 times the pay of their average employee counterparts. These differences have got even bigger yet in the eight intervening years since that was written. Likewise, the average CEO among the Fortune 500 earns as much in a day as their average employee in a year. From a historical perspective, again among the Fortune 500 companies, the pay gap in 2007 was close to ten times as big as it was in 1980s and the gap is still increasing. Boy oh boy, that's quite an incentive to work my way up and away from the front line.

Joking apart, I'm not making a point about who should earn what and what people are worth. That's another book and certainly one I shall not be writing. What I would like to do though, is develop a theme about what direction or route people are subconsciously guided towards, especially if they want to be successful and experience progression.

When it comes to decision-making, I've always found it somewhat strange that important decisions are often made by people that are far removed from the areas that the decision will be ultimately impacting. Again, I know there are other factors such as experience, perspective and oversight that have to be taken into consideration, so it's not as cut and dried as all that. How many large IT programmes have you seen where big decisions are taken, far removed from the front-line; when it finally gets delivered, it just doesn't work well in practice for the operators. Certainly, from an engagement point of view, this can be a major event for people. They now have to work with a new system that is nothing like what they were promised, for the next five years. This doesn't just apply to poor IT directors and CTOs (love you really). It could equally apply to a new expenses process that inadvertently takes so long to fill in, that all hoped for gains are now lost due to the time it takes to fill it in. I'm sure we all have many of our own examples.

It's very hard to make decisions when you are incredibly busy and far removed from the front line, even if you want to get closer. What makes it trickier, is that my remoteness and distance from the areas I am making decision on behalf of, can cushion me from the real impact of my decision-making. In other words, I probably won't get to hear any bad news about the poor decisions I may be making. If or when I get any feedback, it's gone through several management layers and by the time it gets to me, any bad news has been filtered out. No-one likes giving bad news to their boss.

I remember a hilarious and true story where an international bank decided it wanted all of its UK business customers to start using their higher spec international online banking service and stop using the UK system. The changeover involved a massive implementation programme and the deployment of an army of programmers and customer liaison officers. The directive had come right from the top and 'failure was not an option!'

The only slight problem was that the international system didn't calculate VAT (similar to US sales tax), whereas the now obsolete, out-of-favour UK system obviously did. Customers liked the old system; it didn't have all the bells and whistles, but it was reliable, rarely went down and 'did what it said on the tin'. Not surprisingly, when the business banking customers were informed they would be migrated onto the newer system and discovered it didn't calculate the most basic of functions, VAT, they went ballistic and refused to accept it.

Naturally, the poor Liaison officers that took the brunt of the ire and froth, told their local managers that the customers absolutely hated it and weren't going to accept it. Faced with a near revolt on their hands, the local managers went to their area managers and explained that many customers were upset and that some had even indicated they didn't want the newer version. Subsequently, area managers had to gingerly update their bosses on the progress of the Board's 'must do' project: 'There have been one or two hiccups on the way, but that's to be expected. We are slightly behind on the timeline but we've got contingency plans in place'. When the progress update finally made it back up to the board, they were told: 'The plan is on track, the customers love it and this is a good example of how the company is acting in a more joined up way.' Classic!! This is an excellent example of how comfort zones and the fear of disapproval can cause havoc.

To their credit, this story was used in their culture change programme, as an example of how difficult it can be to be open, honest and trusting in a corporate environment. I'll never forget the level of hysteria and hilarity when the top guy recounted the whole sorry tale in front of his troops, hardly able to breathe for laughter. I really thought some people were going to die from excessive guffawing and merriment. Good on him, you don't often encounter that level of courage and humour under such circumstances.

Perhaps more importantly, it shows the difficulties and frailties of making decisions at distance. Our history books are littered with far worse examples of ill-informed plans and war-time blunders that went awry. However, despite the dangers, if you want to play the big boys game, you have to leave the front line and work your way away from it.

Often the best performers are promoted away from frontline. As soon as someone gets good at something, they get bumped up to the next level with an average salary increase of 67%. That's the average jump in remuneration in the UK from being a frontline worker to becoming a first-tier manager. That's a lot of money and a clear incentive to start a journey away from the customer interface.

Sometimes, the pressure is on to meet shareholder returns and costs need to be cut back yet again. Due to the pyramidal shape of many organisations, it's easier and more fruitful to make cuts close to the front line. A head or two here, a packet of biscuits there, the Christmas party budget and the subsidy at the canteen. Unfortunately, these are the things that really matter.

One of the unintended effects of these hierarchical structures that pull people away from the frontline, is to leave the remaining staff on the frontline feeling disenfranchised. They sense where they are is not the best place to be, they are just a cog in a big wheel, at worst 'cannon fodder' or at best a 'staging post'.

From an engagement perspective, this is not good news, as it creates an undercurrent that has to be constantly swam against. Often you hear of companies that have bent over backwards to try to get their staff more engaged, but the engagement figures just don't budge and everyone is left scratching their heads.

More progressive companies have recognized this disadvantageous condition and have taken positive steps to counteract the damaging effect of HQ-centricity. Empowerment, delayering and appropriate decentralization are among a number of strategies that have emerged.

For me, the best antidote to this background disengagement factor has been the implementation of well thought through Lean, Six Sigma and Systems Thinking programmes. Whilst these are tools for process improvement, the philosophy that drives them is much more than that. These approaches if done correctly, literally turn the organisation on its head and prioritise the front line and its interaction with the customer, as the primary focus of attention.

Managers' roles shift from the traditional management of people and resources, using activity measures, and instead focuses their attention on end-to-end service and process flow. This represents a fundamental change in thinking and repositions where decision-making takes place, relative to an organization's customer interfaces.

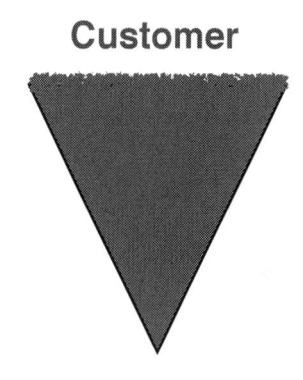

Customer

Staff take on a dual role. One where they carry out their normal duties as before and a second where they work together on improving the service. As a result of this shift, staff themselves re-design and test their own improvements, with managers now in a support role, clearing the path for their changes.

From my own experience with a number of organisations, where done well, this approach has produced significant leaps in performance. Importantly, these improvements have been achieved across all measures, as opposed to one area gaining at the expense of another, as is often the case.

Without doubt though, the real winner is engagement. In the old framework, decision making regarding service improvement lay at the door of the executive, where as now, it lies more firmly in the hands of the people actually delivering the service.

What this means, in human terms, is that people working at the customer interfaces, have an experience of authentic ownership. They fully participate in creating improvements and experience the direct benefits for themselves and their customers, through their own creative input.

'Suddenly the actual work itself becomes engaging and interesting.'

That is a world away from being told what to do, how to do it and then being policed by the all seeing eye of management to do it.

Many organisations recognize the importance of engagement and try to make improvements by focusing on: better communication, better listening, staff suggestion schemes, more flexible hours, better conditions, beautiful offices, making managers responsible for engagement, mentoring, greater mobility and career opportunities, better training, authentic mission statements, internal hires, awards ceremonies and relaxing dress codes. All of these things certainly help and some companies are doing it very well.

Whilst all these things are positive and I whole-heartedly support them, many of them are designed to 'buy' engagement, rather than 'create' it. The truth is, for a lot of people, the nature of the work itself can feel boring, repetitive, uncreative and uninvolving. The reason I like the approach we are discussing here, is that it directly affects the work itself and renders it far more interesting, diverse, creative and participative. Engagement is best created by doing something engaging, especially if you are going to be doing it for a few years.

In the earlier chapter 'The States of Engagement', we explored the idea that engagement is the natural state and maintaining that brilliant state is down to how we manage our responses to 'events'. I am now saying engagement is also about making the work itself engaging. Both are true. Ideally, what you want is engaged people doing engaging things. Now we're talking. This is the space where magic can happen.

Thanking

I like to call the part of our brain that dishes out labels for people (the nice one, the idiot, the creep, my friend, the monster…) the 'Label Production Department'. I didn't realise until later on, that this department is quite a lot larger than I had previously imagined. Labels are not the only product this department specializes in. It is also just as busy in a couple of other lines of business. One of these is called 'Thinging'.

'Thinging' is subtle, but once you learn how to see it, you start notice it everywhere. Primarily, 'thinging' is the process of reducing a live human being into a thing. Let me give you some examples.

You are at the doctors waiting for a flu jab. Then you hear 'next patient please'.
You are at a restaurant and the waiter says 'Who's the fish?'
You are at court in a dispute 'Complainant please step forward'.
You are talking to a colleague and they say 'I see complaints aren't doing very well'.
Someone still owes you £10. When you see them you say to yourself 'Here comes the thief'.
You are a team leader and one of your agents say 'The customer wants a discount'.
You are buying a car in a dealership, you think 'here's the salesman', they think 'heres the punter'.

You may have noticed this before. One second your were an individual human being, the next moment you are now being referred to as a thing, a department or a position. It happens so often, that for the most part it goes on under the radar and we just don't take any notice of it. More often than not, it is just the brains' way of being more efficient and taking short cuts. We often fail to realise however, that this seemingly innocent short-hand is a form of subtle disengagement.
At work, we are surrounded by numbers, metrics, key performance indicators, costs, percentages, volumes, ratios and the rest. If you're not careful, after a while, you even start thinking about people as numbers.

'People become things and everything feels a little impersonal'

There I am, taking calls working in a contact centre. The queue of customers trying to get through to us is horrendous, it never seems to go down. Every day is the same, it's just call, after call, after call. One of the team leaders is strutting around, pointing at the wallboard which tells us 157 customers are still waiting to get through. They screech 'Calls in queue, calls in queue'.

The truth is, those aren't 'calls in queue', those are 'people waiting to speak to us'. However we refer to them as 'calls in queue'. When the customer finally gets through, if we are not careful, they get spoken to as just another call in the queue. At the end of the day, my team leader asks me 'How many calls did you take today?'. I say 'fifty-five'. Perhaps a better question would have been 'How many people did you speak with today?' This is more than mere semantics, this is about how our collective language shapes our experience and the reality we construct for ourselves.

This subtle transition of people into things, depersonalizes our interactions with each other. It makes things feel a bit repetitive and automatic. Customers feel they are treated as just another call, staff feel a little like robots just going through the motions, everything becomes just numbers. We become less present, a little deadened, even numb. In a depersonalized environment, where feelings and responsiveness are dulled, you often hear calls like this:

Customer: 'I've called three times today and each time someone said they would get back to me, and each time they didn't' . I'm not happy at all, what is going on?!'

Agent: [flat tone]'Can I have you account number please'.

Recognize it?

One of the areas this malaise can creep into is in how we thank each other. The limbic brain, as we have discussed, is very concerned with a sense of belonging and feeling valued. It's what cements and confirms our position within our tribe and provides the reassurance we need to satisfy some of our most basic instincts. For this reason, at a fairly subliminal level, we are scanning for signals of acceptance or approval, to validate this experience. Interestingly, the latin root of the word 'praise' means 'to put value on'. Praise is a direct means of affirming that basic desire 'to matter, to make a difference and to be valued'. When done well, praise is powerful medicine indeed. It floods the limbic mind with the good news it's hoping for and most importantly, in the only language it understands: feelings. We have all seen and all felt the power of a well-deserved, sincere thanking. It can keep some people on full power for a good month or two and can even soften the toughest of nuts.

Thanking, in an environment where 'people have becomes things', loses its power and potency. In extreme cases, it may even arouse contrary feelings of cynicism, dismissiveness or even contempt. 'Forget the thanking, just pay me half of what you get!' For thanking to evoke a meaningful positive response, it must affect more than just the logical mind, it has to touch our deeper emotional mind.

I imagine most of us have attended courses and training sessions on praise. Most of the advice is pretty good. 'Timely, specific, sincere, encourage them to do more of the same and don't use it as a sandwich to disguise a criticism.' If we are not careful, the bit that often gets missed out, is the bit that makes the difference.

> *'Say how you feel about what they did.*
> *What difference did it make to you?'*

Allow yourself to enter the Limbic Zone and cross the threshold into the world of emotion. Self-disclose how you feel about it. The difference is tangible.

Here's an example:

'Kate, I listened to one of your calls today. Clearly the customer was upset and was on the verge of leaving us. I thought you handled that complaint really well. Your listening was sincere and accurate and your solution really suited what the customer needed. Your tone was polite throughout. Well done, that was very good'

That's a reasonably good thanking and had most of the elements in place. Listen to this and see if you can 'Feel' the difference.

'Kate, I listened to one of your calls today. Clearly the customer was upset and was on the verge of leaving us. I thought you handled that complaint really well. Your listening was sincere and accurate and your solution really suited what the customer needed. Your tone was polite throughout. **When I heard that call, it made me feel really proud.** *I thought that's just how we should be helping our customers.* **Brilliant, I feel really happy.** *Thank you, well done, that was excellent."*

Good to Great

In recent years, a number of organisations have commenced a journey which they call something along the lines of 'Good to Great' or variants of that. Many organisations find themselves in a position whereby they are neither at the bottom of the competitive leaderboard, nor are they at the top. They are doing well and have made good progress and certainly don't want to discredit or dismiss the progress that has been made to date. However, they are not where they would ideally like to be and want to embark on a journey to 'push for the Summit'.

At the beginning of this decade, a lot of research and study went into determining whether there was a causal link between positivity and subsequent success. This research was primarily spearheaded by doctors Marcial Losada and Emily Heathy.

The first indication of a link between positivity and successful outcomes was discovered in studies conducted by John Gottman, in the area of marriage stability. During his studies, he was careful to ensure his findings were statistically significant and, to this end, repeated them many thousands of times. His observations proved to be so reliable, they allowed him to predict whether or not a couple would divorce with over 90% accuracy. The primary determinant proved to be the ratio of positive expressions to negative ones. In other words, stay engaged and keep those teas coming!

He formulated a simple ratio to express his findings; the number of expressions of positivity divided by the number of negative ones. A ratio of 3:1 up to 6:1 was found to be the 'sweet spot'.

In studies conducted on nominally 'Good' companies, compared to their 'Great' counterparts, they discovered that the highest-performing companies tended to display about three times as many expressions of positivity to boost performance, as their medium-performing opposite numbers.

Often, praise is reserved for exceptional behaviour or efforts beyond the call of duty. If we think about it though, to get anywhere near the suggested number of six positives to every negative, we are going to have to start to look in some different places. Either that or never say anything negative at all! I'm certainly not going to be suggesting that. To get into the prescribed 3:1- 6:1 zone, or anywhere near it, requires moving into 'business as usual' areas and pro-actively going on the hunt for good news. Personally, I'm not a big fan of precise mathematical formulas being applied to what are essentially issues of emotion. However, it is quite clear that a significant shift toward more thanking could pay real dividends. Some people may baulk at the idea. However, I put it to you, I don't think there are that many people out there who are suffering from too much praise. Maybe it's true for the odd celebrity, adulation-hungry magnate or daughter that has daddy wrapped around her little finger, but for the most of us, too much praise is not something we lose sleep over.

Engaging and thanking at an emotional level will help counteract the background numbing effect of numbers, 'thinging' and depersonalization.

I once ran the back office area of a large organisation. There were about five hundred of us and I was the new boy. I decided on a simple policy of getting to know every one by name and taking the long way around to my desk in the morning. This meant I could make as much contact with everyone as possible, before I started my day. This seemed to go down very well, so I thought I would take it to the next level. Each week, I would get in especially early on the Monday morning, to ensure I was first in. I would greet each and every person as they walked in through the front door. In addition to that, on the Friday afternoon, I would position myself by the very same door. I would shake everyone's hand as they left for the day and thank them for their weeks work, irrespective of how well they had done.

At first and not unexpectedly, it drew a few funny looks and expressions of surprise. I'm sure one or two thought I was a very strange man indeed. After time though, this became a ritual we all looked forward to and it was the thing I received most positive feedback on. In some way, it seemed to connect us all and the whole experience of working there felt lighter and more human. I like to think that the tremendous rapport we built in that office spilled out onto our customers and colleagues. The results certainly seemed to suggest so.

There was one occasion when I was stuck in an internal meeting on a Friday afternoon. A few colleagues, unannounced, pushed their way into the room and absolutely insisted I stand by the front door to see everyone out. In a funny way, that was one the highlights of my career. They really let me get to them and I really let them get to me. It didn't feel like work after that.

Growing

Experiencing a strong sense of personal satisfaction is an excellent way to maintain and improve our experience of engagement. In particular, it improves our resilience to negative experiences that may otherwise take us towards a path of increasing disengagement.

When I say personal satisfaction, I do not mean it in a selfish way. Much satisfaction, in fact some would argue, the greatest satisfaction comes through helping and satisfying the needs of others.

As we all know, the experience of satisfaction can be achieved through short-term materialistic gain. Much of today's consumerism is based on this principle. Advertising and marketing campaigns cash in on it very successfully. Many of us however, are very familiar with the law of diminishing returns and are well aware that these short term solutions, whilst great at the time, are not necessarily a lasting route to satisfaction.

There are a number of activities that create longer term satisfaction and can be incorporated into how we interact with our colleagues and the people around us:

  Breakthrough/growth
  Making a contribution/helping others
  Being part of something with an exciting purpose
  Creating something exceptional
  Closing the gap between who you are and what you do
  Completing incompletions
  Putting in 100%

Few things cause greater satisfaction than 'Breakthrough' and 'Personal Growth'. The two are closely related to each other and both involve breaking through the confines of our comfort zones.

As we discussed in the section on Comfort Zones, 'what's scary' isn't being outside of our comfort zone necessarily, 'what's scary' is being in your comfort zone and thinking about leaving it. The scariness is more a product of our overactive imagination, rather than the actual experience of being outside of our zone.

Let's go back to the story of standing up in front of the three hundred unhappy customers. If we carefully examine the timeline from the point of invitation up until just after the big event itself, what we discover is that the peak of anxiety and nervousness often occurs just prior to the point when I have to stand up. Once I am standing up and starting to interact, it starts to progressively ease. Many people have reported this phenomenon, it's not uncommon at all, far from it. It's not the 'doing it' that's the problem, it's the thinking about doing it. I'm sure you have had this experience too.

One of the reasons for this is down to where our attention is placed. In the hours, minutes and moments leading up to the event, my attention is progressively focused inwards on myself. I know this because the voice in my head is getting progressively louder, busier and obsessive. I am becoming increasingly aware of the feelings and sensations in my body and my energy is focussed inwards. The voice in my head seems louder than those of other people, making listening difficult. I think we all laugh at those comic moments on TV when someone is told the worst possible news and they can't hear anything for a few seconds. All they can see is mouths moving but no sound. It's funny because it's true. You can see when other people are nervous, their energy, attention and focus is all directed back into themselves.

At the point at which I have to stand up and start interacting, the dynamic changes. My attention shifts from being on myself and moves progressively onto the other people in the room. As soon as this happens, the uncomfortable feelings gradually start to subside.

I am now outside of my comfort zone, interacting, participating and doing my best to answer some tricky questions. It slowly starts working and in our example, it ends up in a good place. I have achieved 'Breakthrough'. I am operating at a higher level and have gone beyond what I thought was possible. The resulting sense of satisfaction is intense and will stay with me for quite some time. I will probably use this experience as a source of courage and determination for the future and especially when I come up against my next big challenge.

The net effect is my comfort zone has expanded. With this expansion, a whole bucket-load of positive emotion is released. I feel more confident, more courageous. I feel bigger and more able. Suddenly, everything feels more possible. Some people climb mountains to capture that experience. I managed it in a hotel conference room.

The great thing about comfort zones is that an expansion in one area can positively affect many other areas. I'm sure we've all felt that. Many people target breakthrough in sports or personal fitness, as they know progress in these ares will spill over into other areas of their lives. Regular breakthrough can yield very positive outcomes, particularly in the area of your mind set, resilience against negativity and general overall positivity. The opposite is also true. If someone goes for extended periods of no breakthrough, it has the opposite effect. The problem is, comfort zones are not static, they are either growing or shrinking. Turning down opportunities to breakthrough, will cause your comfort zone to shrink.

An expanding or shrinking comfort zone exhibits symptoms and tendencies which influence our choices, actions and behaviours. In many cases, they also determine how we feel and how we imagine things will turn out. Here are a few examples, there are many more.

EXPANDING	SHRINKING

Open to new ideas and challenges	Suspicious of anything new
Optimistic about how things will turn out	Pessimistic about how things may turn out
A feeling of forward movement	A sense of going backwards
Becoming more yourself	A feeling of not being yourself
Feeling buoyant and confident	Moody or even grumpy
Less subject to fear or anxieties	Affected by concerns or imagined fears

Bert was very aware of the importance of ensuring his people experienced themselves as growing and expanding. He knew the inherent problems associated with a lack of challenge and regular breakthrough and the diminished mindsets that comes with that. When it came to goal setting and delegating various tasks and challenges, he'd take these moments particularly seriously. He would take care to ensure each was turned into an opportunity, to promote breakthrough.

On receipt of their goal from their boss, some managers take the target, divide it by the number of people in their team and pass it on. Some will even build in a buffer to ensure they get their goal, even if some members of the team don't get theirs. Very little attention is given to how this target can be set as a context for breakthrough.

One of the reasons I undoubtably knew Bert's motive was to grow me, was in the way he set my goals and delegated various tasks to me. He always made absolutely sure, whatever I took on, that it lay just outside my comfort zone and would stretch me. He wanted to know that to achieve it, I would have to breakthrough my own limitations or barriers. Sometimes, he didn't tell me what goal he wanted me to take on, quite often he'd tell me what his goal was and then ask me what I thought I'd like to achieve. Either way, he'd stick to his principle of growth. It wasn't always comfortable working with Bert, in fact sometimes quite the opposite. Without doubt however, it was incredibly satisfying, especially when you saw other members of the team breaking through to new levels as well.

After a while, you get used to your own mind and how it works when faced with a new, 'outside of the comfort zone' challenges. You start to get good at identifying 'reasons' and 'excuses' and treat them for what they are, just 'imagined survival' and press on anyway.

Some managers target comfort and won't do anything to push themselves or anyone else near the edge of their comfort zone. They avoid causing any emotion or sensation. The trouble is, as well as avoiding the difficult experiences, you end up avoiding the good ones too. All you end up with is 'numb'. I personally consider that a disservice.

> 'Good managers are willing to have feelings.
> Great managers are willing to cause them'.

I joined Bert a manager, a year later I left him a director. The Bert Diet certainly worked for me.

Social Dimension

'We human beings are social beings. We come into the world as the result of others' actions. We survive here in dependence on others. Whether we like it or not, there is hardly a moment of our lives when we do not benefit from others' activities. For this reason, it is hardly surprising that most of our happiness arises in the context of our relationships with others.'
His holiness, Dalai Lama XIV

The same message is strongly reinforced by our scientific community. They also conclude that as human beings, we are deeply social beings. From an evolutionary perspective, this social nature proved to be highly advantageous. Instead of evolving claws, teeth or talons, humanity adapted towards 'collaborative society' as its preferred method for hunting, defence from predators and bringing up our young. It gave us the ability to not only create tools and knowledge, but to share and develop that knowledge and pass it down to later generations. This strategy to depart from brute strength and evolve socially has proved to be unusually successful and led to the extraordinary ascent of man. Collaboration and engagement is literally woven into our DNA.

To a great extent, modern living has prompted work to become one of, if not, the main place where we now gather and congregate. Alongside this however, due to the continual need to make a short-term profit, many organisations have slipped into viewing their workforce as a cost. These two trends don't sit well together, especially where cost-reduction becomes the overt primary motive and productivity gains are often single-mindedly policed and monitored.

For many, outside of financial security or progression, the laughs, the banter, the chats and the friendships are what make work so rewarding, or at least tolerable. Unfortunately, the social dimension tends to suffer, where the desire to engage with each other at work is seen at odds with productivity gains. 'Chatting about holiday snaps is bad, looking busy is good'.

'Engagement is a state, not a thing. A bit like happiness, if it is suppressed or controlled in one area, it tends to affect the whole. No-one will engage fully with the business or its customers, if they are not allowed to engage with each other.'

More enlightened organisations recognize the importance of the social dimension and seek to resolve the profit motive with engendering and promoting a more activated social aspect to the business. Some would even say that the social dimension is a positive driver of profit, as opposed to the opposite.

'Millennials' or 'Generation Y', as they are sometimes called, now make up approximately one third of todays working population. Millennials were typically born in the early 1980's and 2000. By 2020 they will make up about 50% of the talent pool and by 2025 a whopping 75%. Whilst I am no believer in gross generalizations, there are some quite observable differences between their predecessors; The Baby Boomers (1946-64) and Generation X (1965-84). Some of these traits relate directly to the workplace and are worthy of mention:
- Millennials want communication from the boss more frequently than any other generation in the workforce - up to 54%. [The Centre for Generational Kinetics]
- They want to be allowed to provide more input, not simply be given input from the top.
- They want to know they have a voice at the table
- They want collaborative environments

- 65% said personal development was the most influential factor in their current job, mentoring was particularly popular
- 64% ask about social media policies during interviews
- Beyond just work life balance, many want a more unified balance; more lounge areas, places to meditate, access to better food and greater opportunity to be with work colleagues

Have you created an environment that maximizes the social dimension? Is your business more than just work? Is it somewhere where people look forward to going to? Does your business promote friendship? Do you want people to engage with each other?

My personal mission in life, apart from making cups of tea, has been to 'humanize commerce'. I have always hated stale, lifeless, environments and have sought to inject the 'human touch', wherever I possibly can. In my entire experience, I have never seen productivity drop off because we were having too much fun, in fact, quite the opposite. 'Fun is bad' is an old idea and has not stood the test of time. Chuck it out I say!

One of the best things I have seen on my travels is what I call the 'Ministry of Fun'. A 'Ministry of Fun' is simply a small group of people that are responsible for introducing a bit of fun into the day. It doesn't have to look any particular way, but there are a few simple rules:

1. The ministers are freely chosen by the people, not the managers.
2. They are usually voted in purely on the basis of who we think is 'Funny' and seem to be good at making people laugh.
3. No one has to get involved in what the ministry devises, it is purely voluntary.

If you ever find yourself getting voted in as a Minister, firstly: congratulations! That's a great bit of feedback! Secondly, quite a lot of people are not necessarily used to having much fun at work and will deal with this little change in many different ways. Some will look at you as if you are an idiot, others will accuse you of being childish or silly and one or two will say you are stopping people from working. That is par for the course. My advice would be: take no offence, refrain from dishing out negative labels and focus purely on the open doors. They will join in when they are good and ready and that's fine. What you will be doing though, is steadily building the social dimension of the group and you will be amazed what that will do for productivity, sickness levels and staff turnover.

The Art of Engagement

'and that's all I have to say about that...'
Forrest Gump

Enchantment is a wonderful thing, you never really quite know when or where it is going to turn up next. It can literally come from anywhere. As I write, my most recent moment of enchantment came from 'The Graham Norton Show', (a UK Friday night BBC chat show). I don't watch chat shows as a rule, but this one was particularly good. One of the guests was the inimitable Tom Hanks, one of my favourite actors. Amongst other things, he was talking about his new upcoming film. The interview covered the usual topics and then magically settled on one that really put a huge ear-to-ear smile on my face. They were discussing the famous Forrest Gump accent, which in a way added the magical ingredient to the film and in particular, where it came from. Tom Hanks described the wonderful story of how he was introduced to a young Michael Conner Humphreys. He was to play the eight-year old 'Gump' in leg braces. Michael Connor Humphreys was from deep Mississippi and had that now famous strong southern accent with a hard 'g' at the end of some of his sen-ten-ces.

The director, a concerned Robert Zemeckis apparently said to Tom, 'We've got a problem on this. You're going to have to teach this kid to talk like you!'

Tom Hanks, in a moment of pure selflessness said 'Why don't I just talk the way that he talks right now?' He then spent hours and hours with a tape recorder perfecting the accent, which we all know and love to this day. What a great story! The mighty Tom Hanks, with two Oscars, seven Emmy awards, a BAFTA and four Golden Globes, chose to go totally out of his way and accommodate a young eight year old kid.

In my way of seeing things, that wonderful accent didn't just come from Mississippi, it came from a lack of ego. The Art of Engagement is summed up in heart of that little story, the simple moment of choice, the simple act of getting over yourself and choosing to do the right thing.

When difficult events turn up that make it a little harder to stay on the path of engagement, we are all faced with a choice. We either allow ourselves to go down the path of disengagement, assign blame and negative labels or, we catch ourselves out and return to our positive true selves.

My great friend Tony faced such choice very recently. His ex-wife died suddenly, leaving four lovely boys at vulnerable ages. He could easily have crumpled, but he chose to fully engage and and become the 'super-dad' they all so badly needed. Tony rose to meet adversity, face-to-face and the glint is back in his eye.

React or Respond?

The Art of Engagement lies in our ability to respond to events rather than react to them.

When we **react** to events we don't like the look of, our automatic limbic system goes into defence mode. We immediately blame the event for making us feel a certain way and feel justified about our negative opinions, labels and beliefs. We are on automatic and we are too busy blaming our circumstances and other people to notice we are well on our way down the the path of disengagement.

When we **respond** to events, we simply catch ourselves out reacting. This simple awareness is all it takes to notice we are having an automatic reaction and it affords us a few more moments to make better choices.

Here are three little steps devised by my friend Woody to help you back to the path of engagement when an event strikes.

1. Notice: 'aha, **I'm** having a reaction'
2. Respond by deciding what outcome you really want…'Ideally, I want to stay engaged'
3. Be how you'd be if you were fully engaged and do what you'd do if you were fully engaged.

More often than not, this will work perfectly and will return you swiftly back to your original positivity.

If it doesn't, by all means, choose to fully communicate to resolve the issue or if really necessary, you can leave

With a bit of practice, this becomes a habit and catching yourself out becomes routine. Lesser people than Tom Hanks could easily have reacted and thrown a diva-fit. 'Get me someone who can talk properly. Who the hell cast this role. I'm going to my trailer!!". He didn't, he responded and made magic.

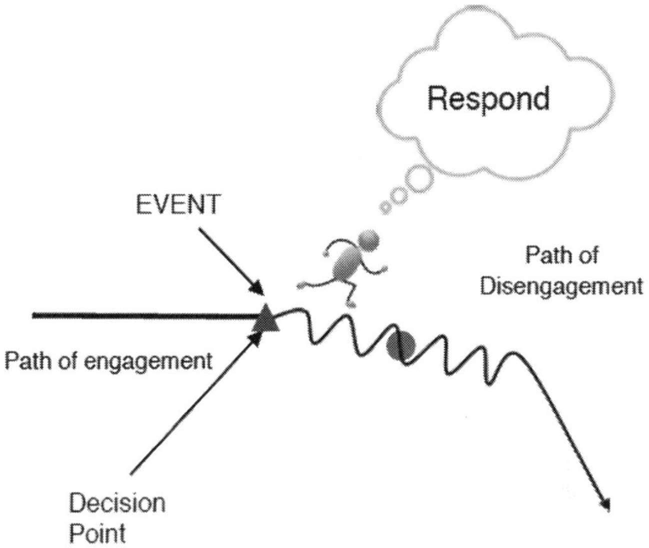
Respond
EVENT
Path of
Disengagement
Path of engagement
Decision
Point

Disengaged people don't exist. That's just an unimaginative way of viewing the situation. Everyone is an 'A'. I am, you are. We are simply people wanting to discover just how big we can really be. Don't settle for numbness or cruise-control. Practice the 'Art of Engagement' and grow yourself a field of bamboo.

'That's all I have to say about that...'

Resources

the McLeod review web links http://dera.ioe.ac.uk/1810/1/file52215.pdf

Videos and TED Talks

Simon Sinek - 'How great leaders inspire action'. https://www.ted.com/talks/simon_sinek_how_great_leaders_inspire_action?language=en

The Graham Norton Show and the interview with Tom Hanks https://www.youtube.com/watch?v=QmMHP6JxU4s

Further reading: NLP books

Introducing NLP by Joseph O'Connor and John Seymour

NLP at work by Sue Knight

Influencing with integrity by Genie Z. Laborde

For UK NLP courses, contact Zetetic Pioneering Strategies www.zeteticmind.com

The next step

If you are interested to take these ideas further, or would like assistance to improve engagement levels within your own organisation, please feel free to contact me by email or via my website.

I am available for:

Speaking engagements
Free talk and book signing events for your team or business
Leadership workshops or executive coaching

Contact

david@goodhabits.org.uk
www.goodhabits.org.uk

Printed in Great Britain
by Amazon